Advance Praise for Formula X

"A faster organization is a struggle for many companies. Formula X is an amazing book that makes clear that you learn easiest from companies outside of your market, instead of your competitors. The way this book explains how to increase the speed and ultimately the success of an organization is unique and stimulating for anyone who wants to lead a faster team or organization."

— **Harry Brouwer – CEO, Unilever Food Solutions**

"There is a strong relationship between the challenges faced in this story and what I encounter in my own job. Drawing patterns in problems allows me to abstract the issue and apply logic to necessary changes. The underlying model was the highlight of the book for me. Professionals need to understand and master this theory."

— **Jeff Willard – Director of Global Network Services, Nike**

"Faced with the need for acceleration in organizations, this book is accessible to all and contains smart, useful tools. Let's get started!"

— **Wilma van Dijk – Director of Safety, Security & Environment, Amsterdam Airport Schiphol**

"A great handbook and source of inspiration to make our organization agile. I learned a lot from the many examples of how to do this effectively. Formula X teaches you how to turn your organization into a learning machine. This beautiful book contains many practical solutions that help get an organization moving and, above all, keep it moving. Recommended for people with a passion for change!"

— **Amir Arooni – CIO, NN Group**

"*Formula X* reads like an exciting adventure, full of insights for organizations that want to move faster and act more decisively. The key message is that self-managing, multidisciplinary teams, focusing on clear goals and on continuous innovation and value creation, will become winners for the customer. Leaders can take away a law of nature by understanding how weight and inertia will slow you down and that diversity, rhythm, and rituals help to make teams stronger and perform better. A good formula for learning organizations in dynamic markets!"

— Jeroen Tas – Chief Innovation & Strategy Officer, Philips

"Finally a book that offers guidelines on how to make your organization truly agile. Although a lot has been written about agile and scrum, there is still little to be found about how to *organize* it. *Formula X* changes that. This book shows how to look at your organization differently. Jurriaan and Rini have articulated this in a very readable book. I read it in one sitting and am already applying the lessons! Change starts with ourselves: how we look at our organization, how we look at our people, how to empower people and work towards a common goal. This book is an absolute must!"

— Frank Coster – CIO, Randstad Group NL

"*Formula X* describes, in a playful way, how organizations can become agile and effective by distributing decision-making and building on trust and real cooperation in a safe environment. This fits in with the way we want to work at bol.com and it takes us further."

— Huub Vermeulen – CEO, www.bol.com

"This book is a page-turner! One of the most important insights for me is that, as a leader, I have to change. Trust instead of control. Making mistakes is fine if you learn from them. Tap into the thinking power of everyone instead of just the management team. And the best result, besides acceleration, is very happy people!"

— Mariëlle Lichtenberg – Director of Consumers, Rabobank

THE
FORMULA X
EXPERIENCE

A full-day immersive workshop facilitated by authors Jurriaan Kamer and Rini van Solingen. Go above and beyond everything you've learned from this book and kickstart extreme acceleration in your organization. In this highly interactive experience we will work with your team(s) to unlock long-lasting speed and agility.

Get inspired by F1 and other modern organizations
Learn and apply the FASTER model
Reflect on the current way of working
Design tangible improvements
Make personal commitments
Receive expert advice and follow-up materials
Suggested location: a go-kart or race track

Location: a go-kart or race track

www.formula-x.co/workshop

Jurriaan Kamer
Rini van Solingen

Formula X

How to reach extreme acceleration in your organization

– A Business Fable –

© 2020 Jurriaan Kamer en Rini van Solingen

Cover design by Adept Vormgeving

ISBN: 978-1-95-036722-1

www.formula-x.co

"If everything seems under control, you're not going fast enough!"

Mario Andretti (former Formula 1 driver)

Contents

The Fable

Prologue

After the echo of the slamming front door has faded away, it suddenly becomes quiet in the house. Is this what I want? Is this all worth it?

Then my phone rings. An unknown number. I reject the call. A few seconds later, the phone rings again. I reject it again, but I get called back immediately. Ugh. Though I'm irritated, I decide to take the call.

"Hi, this is Ronald Park." On the other side, I hear a rumbling sound and some music. I can't make sense of it...until I hear a voice: "Hello, hello? This is me, can you hear me? Can you come to London? I need to speak to you urgently." I recognize that voice. It's Hank, my company's founder, and majority shareholder. He sounds confused and drunk. And panicked. Of course, I will go. Through thick and thin, I'm always there for Hank. I get into my car quickly and drive to London, about an hour away.

I finally see him and immediately notice that he's in complete despair. "I've worked very hard all these years. But it has been for nothing!" It's very unlike him to act from a place of anguish.

"Hank, what do you mean? What's the matter? Why are you panicking?"

"Did you really not see this coming, Ronald?! My money has almost run out in the last few months. I'm close to bankruptcy. There is only money left for a few weeks. I kept depositing money from my own pocket, but we're close to hitting rock bottom!"

He continues: "I can already see the headlines: 'From Multi-Millionaire to Welfare Recipient.'" He becomes silent and stares straight ahead. I am puzzled and don't know what to say. Then he suddenly looks at me and grabs my shoulders firmly. With his arms outstretched, he looks me in the eye as he begs me: "You are the only one who can get us out of this, Ronnie. Will you please help? Only you can save us!"

PART ONE

Free Practice

Nine months earlier

Quickie

*Nine months earlier, on a
Saturday afternoon in March*

"onald, why don't you do anything about it? You are the managing director, aren't you?" my wife Emily shouts annoyedly from the living room couch. I'm in the kitchen making an espresso. She's never been a big fan of our company's commercials, but this one she really hates. "This is really unacceptable! That commercial is really very sexist!"

I met Emily when I studied logistics in London. We both lived in the same student apartment. The first time I saw her, I was head over heels. It really was love at first sight from my side. But not for Emily. She had built a wall around her to counter all the advances of testosterone-rich students. I persisted for a long time. I sent her flowers, love letters, chocolate, and roses. Eventually, she gave in and went out with me. The same month we canceled our student apartments and rented a flat together. After we graduated, we got married.

Our founder, Hank Rapid, is the leading actor in our commercial. He is dressed like a cowboy: bare torso, brown boots underneath his jeans and he wears a large gray cowboy hat on his head. His long gray hair hangs down in a ponytail. In the commercial, he shows off his tanned and hairy chest. Hank is already in his late sixties, but I must admit that he looks a lot younger with his slender and muscular build.

His arms are wrapped around the waists of two sultry models. Both are dressed in workwear from our company, but...let's just say it was a short-skirt version of our workwear. The girls look into the camera rather seductively, each with a hand on Hank's bare chest.

With a big smile, he says: "Howdy! Here I am again: Kitchen Cowboy. Do you want a new kitchen but don't have a lot of time? Then quickly go to the Kitchen Quick website. We specialize in fast and very satisfactory delivery. So, fancy a quickie? Go to kitchen-quick.com!" Hank gives a big smile, the models both give him a kiss on the cheek, and the commercial ends.

The commercial is designed to be annoying and borderline inappropriate. That's why it stands out. I suggested to Hank that we make it more professional, but he politely declined my suggestion. "It sells, right?" was his response. And...he's right. The more media buzz about our ads, the more orders come in.

It's been four years since Hank asked me to come and work for him at Kitchen Quick. I was ready for something new after working for more than eight years at a large supermarket chain in various management positions. There was constant pressure to climb the corporate ladder, and I grew fed up with its "up or out" culture.

So I hired a career coach. He advised me to look outside of the corporate world and consider joining smaller companies. He put me in touch with one of his business contacts: Kitchen Quick. Kitchen Quick is a British company with an American shareholder.

I decided to apply for the role of CEO. I think Hank took a bit of a risk to hire me: I was in my twenties and had no experience in the kitchen business. Hank is someone who looks at potential, and I'm fortunate he saw that in me.

In the beginning, I had to get used to him. He is a flamboyant man who gets what he wants. "I always do what others think is impossible" is his motto. He is stubborn, smart, and spry. A true entrepreneur. Someone who sees money-making opportunities everywhere. And he's successful. He was a multi-millionaire before he was thirty. And he loves to brag about that. I think it's because of his American roots. He usually wears extravagant and eye-catching clothes. He owns a large collection of shiny leather shoes in the craziest colors, like bright pink and bright green. And I must admit: they look good on him! Especially with his tanned face and a beautiful head of long gray hair.

Hank wanted to take a step back from the daily management of the company. The house (as he always calls it) pretty much ran itself. He didn't go to the office that much anymore; he was busy with all sorts of new start-ups. I think he eventually got bored with running Kitchen Quick. "I want a managing director to look after my pension" was his main motivation to hire me.

To take this job we had to move from our apartment close to Holland Park in London to a house in the Kent Countryside. For Emily, moving was not such a problem. As an interim HR manager, she is used to having assignments throughout the country. And I was quite eager to live in a more rural area: a pleasant environment to raise children if we ever wanted to start a family.

Emily and I often have conversations about whether we should have children. Emily has always wanted two kids. She is just thirty-one, a few years younger than me. And now that her younger sister had a baby, she has been talking more and more about raising a child. I also really want a family. But I also realize it is an irreversible decision. And we still have so many plans: traveling, building successful careers, maybe even living abroad for a few years. Also, just a few weeks ago, Emily started a degree in organizational consulting. She notices that the role of an HR manager is changing considerably. Nowadays, there is a lot of demand for freelancers with knowledge of new ways of organizing. Therefore, I believe it is a good idea if she completes her career switch before we have children. I think she should first complete her education, because knowing Emily, both at the same time would be too much for her.

Anyway, back to my job as a managing director at Kitchen Quick. If I took the job, I'd have to accept a 30 percent drop in salary compared to my previous job. Therefore, I asked Hank if I could get stock options. In the long run, he would consider doing that, but not immediately from the start. "You have to earn it first," he said. And I respected that. We agreed to discuss it later.

I also find our ads quite annoying. I agree with Emily that they are rather sexist. I don't have trouble with the intent of our ads: they stand out and generate business. What I have trouble with is what they promise.

The Kitchen Cowboy asserts that we can install a "quickie" kitchen, but that is not true at all! On average we install a kitchen in roughly twelve weeks. Sometimes a bit faster, but often longer as well. It's not a huge problem, given that our competitors have similar delivery times, but raising the expectations through this ad gives us zero benefits: we just disappoint our customers.

Before I became CEO, Hank tried to shorten the delivery time but he failed. He achieved a few small improvements in the process, but the total delivery time continued to be roughly three months. This frustrated Hank immensely. And that is not surprising, as he is extremely impatient by nature.

If Hank has a new idea, he expects others to be able to implement it within a few hours. He has no sense of time at all. He doesn't seem to want to understand that some things can take weeks to months before they have changed. That's why many of his plans fail. By the time a new idea is implemented, he already has a new one. Long-term employees are used to this. Often when Hank proposes something, they initially do nothing, as they know it is a matter of time before Hank changes his mind again.

This makes my work more difficult because when I ask an employee to do something, I always have to check whether he or she actually does it. I really want to have faith in my people, but I learned through experience that that is not enough. I always tell my managers: "Trust is good, but control is better!"

I didn't suspect that this attitude will almost lead to our downfall...

To the Office

Monday morning – a working day like so many

Because I have an appointment in the evening, I drive my car to the office. In total, Kitchen Quick has four showrooms spread across the country. However, most of the time I can be found in our head office where the kitchens are also manufactured. I park my car in the parking lot behind the building. In the past, there were a few private parking lots for executives, right next to the front door. Hank liked to park his expensive cars there. "That's to make sure people can see things are going very well here" was his main argument. But I disagreed; I thought it was a sign for suppliers that they didn't have to skimp on their prices. "Plenty of money here" it radiated to me.

When I was initially appointed as managing director, I asked for the results of the employee satisfaction survey. It turned out that the executive parking lots were an eyesore for several people. I could totally relate, as in my previous job I had always been annoyed by the privileges that executives were given. The board even had its own elevator that took them directly from the parking garage to their "executive" floor. In other words: I don't want executive parking places in my company. Hank didn't like my decision at all but he didn't interfere. After all, he promised to hand over the day-to-day-decision making to me.

I walk the same walk every morning I arrive. I greet the receptionists at the entrance. Then I turn to the right on to the production floor: the heart of our company. Here is where the kitchens are produced. It is full of sawing machines and all kinds of other equipment. It is a bit messy; there is sawdust everywhere, and it always smells wonderfully of freshly sawn wood. Around thirty people work there. I recognize all of their faces and know most of their names. Yet they all look quite similar in their overalls. And they all talk similarly. It is often difficult to have a casual chat because everyone is wearing ear protection to combat the sawing machine noise.

In the middle of the production floor, next to the coffee machine, is Thom's office. He is the manager of the production floor. Thom has been trying for years to get an office on our second floor, but I don't allow it. I believe the Head of Production should be on the production floor, among his people. As I walk past Thom's office, I knock on the window and wave hi. Thom is busy.

Thom is as tall as a tree. Over two meters high, and he has a very large nose. He has recently turned fifty-five but he still looks quite young for his age. There is no trace of gray in his black curly hair. Rumor has it that he dyes it, but he firmly denies that.

When Kitchen Quick was founded over thirty years ago, Thom was one of the first employees. At the time he was nicknamed "The Saw." Several years later, he was promoted to manager. If you see him today, you wouldn't guess that he started as a carpenter. For example, he always wears a suit. I think that's a bit strange for a Head of Production. The production floor is very dusty, so I think it's a waste of such good clothes. Although I believe everyone should be able to decide what they want to wear.

Thom is very hands-on with the people he manages. He believes workers are lazy by nature and a necessary evil. They don't deliver the required quality level and they never do exactly what you have in mind. They always make a crucial mistake or call in sick just at the wrong time. I think that is nonsense and often argue with him about this mindset.

From the production floor, I walk to the other side of the building where I grab the elevator to the third floor. This is where customer service is seated, a large department that increasingly starts to look like a professional call center: a large room with people sitting behind computer screens, wearing headsets. Everyone is chattering all the time to the point where it eerily resembles a chicken coop. I often wonder how people are able to do their work, with so much noise around them. Fortunately, customers on the phone hear nothing of the ambient noise.

I run into Laura: the customer service manager. She is very good at her job and is often on the phone herself to help customers. Laura has a high-pitched voice that is friendly but also penetrating. She has long blond hair and black glasses. We hired her shortly after she obtained her communications degree. She is super smart and was promoted to manager of her department within a few years. She is the definition of "customer obsessed." When managing the day-to-day affairs, we are often focused on ourselves, but Laura keeps everyone sharp to keep the customer at the center. Laura is also a bit of an iconoclast. She isn't afraid to raise issues and often challenges other people's opinions. I really love that we have someone with her character on our management team!

Next to customer service is the canteen. It is a nice, spacious room with lots of daylight. Everyone fits in during lunch so we don't have to break for lunch in shifts, which is convenient. We recently updated the furniture. We also often use the canteen when there is something to celebrate. For example, I recently put Thom in the spotlight when he had his thirty-year job anniversary.

I walk through the canteen to the Installation department. Wilma is in charge here. Her department ensures that the kitchens are installed and fitted in the customers' homes. Because every house and kitchen is different, the work involves a lot of customization.

Wilma is very friendly, a real "people person." I'm not a huge fan of that expression, but "people person" really suits her. She wants the best for everyone. She cares for her people incredibly well. She even keeps records of the birthdays of all her employees and even their loved ones. Amazingly, she sends personalized gifts when an employee's partner or kid has their birthday!

Although Placement is the largest department of our company, they have the least number of workplaces in the building. The installers are almost never in the office. When they do come to the office, it is to pick up kitchens and materials and load them in their vans. Then they are quickly gone again, on their way to the customer.

A while ago, Wilma moved her workplace to the production floor, right next to Thom. This way she could easily see her people when they walked in to load things. But that was a disaster. Wilma and Thom are really opposites. Within moments they were bickering about the smallest things, so Wilma decided to move back to the third floor.

After a short conversation with Wilma about the ongoings of her department, I walk down the stairs to the second floor. There I have a chat with my two colleagues from Finance and HR.

I continue walking to see if Paul is present, our sales and planning director. He manages all salesmen in our showrooms. Paul is a slick guy, a true salesman. Always wears a tight suit and has product in his hair. He has a big smile with snow-white teeth. He is proud of his watch, which is just a little too big, and drives a caddish BMW. I know some colleagues call him "Mr. Teflon" behind his back. At the same time, everyone respects Paul. Nobody calls him that when he's present.

Paul isn't here this morning. But his colleagues from the planning department are. They convert customer orders into workorders for production. They ensure all materials are on time and the production process runs smoothly. They also plan the installation of the kitchens. They are regularly in touch with the customer. This sometimes leads to discussions about who should be responsible for customer contact: Should it be planning or Laura's customer service department?

I don't mind that Paul isn't in the office. His main responsibility is to ensure that sales go well, and that happens in the showrooms. When I see him in the office for two consecutive days, I tease him by saying that he apparently has already achieved his monthly target. He doesn't mind; we joke around a lot. He is verbally sharp and witty. Those are important qualities for a salesman.

Paul believes that customers should give us as much money as possible and as quickly as possible. He doesn't mind pressuring customers into closing the deal. Unfortunately, that has an impact on the customer experience. Buying a kitchen is really different from shopping in the supermarket. It is a considerable investment and it is a product that you want to enjoy for a long time. So not something you quickly decide on. At the same time, we know that if customers leave the showroom without ordering, it is likely they won't return. Therefore when the customer is in our showroom, we try to tempt them to make a quick decision, with an extra discount or free kitchen equipment.

I heard Paul is currently working on a very special project. He can't say much about it because he signed a non-disclosure agreement—one that's ten pages with major penalty clauses. This is because it concerns a possible order from the royal family. Hank had received the lead from a golf friend and passed it on to Paul. Exciting! It would be stellar if Paul is able to close this deal.

Next to Paul's office is my spacious office. I have a large wooden desk and a private conference table with chairs. From my window, I look at a number of other office buildings, so that's not really inspiring. To compensate for that, I have a large photo with the New York skyline on my wall. I would love to live there someday.

Kitchen Slow

The phone on my desk is ringing. I recognize the number. It is Hank, our sleeping shareholder. Well, at least that's what he's supposed to be. In practice, it is difficult for him to let go. He calls me a few times a week, and I'm also aware he regularly contacts other colleagues. Fortunately, he is often abroad, so most of our contact is over the phone.

I answer the phone. Hank immediately says: "Hey, Ronnie, listen. A friend of mine spoke to me at the golf club last week. He told me that he bought a kitchen from us a few months ago for his new home. Because of our relationship, he decided we should be the first choice. Unfortunately, he told me a terrible story about what he experienced as a customer."

That doesn't sound good. I listen closely as he continues: "At first he and his wife were very impressed with the service. They were offered apple pie, soup, and sandwiches upon entering. It went down from there. Figuring out the kitchen wasn't easy: endless possibilities and options. He then mentioned that he wanted to sleep on it, but the salesmen didn't allow them to. He pressured them: if they would sign today, they would get a 30 percent discount and they would get the kitchen equipment for free. And he told them the offer really was only valid on that day. This convinced them to go ahead. When they finally made all the choices and placed the order, they were very relieved. They were ready to get out of there after signing the papers. But then, he heard that the delivery time of the kitchen was over three months!

Three f*cking months!! They didn't anticipate this amount of time, and it was a disaster because they were soon given the key to their new home and wanted to move in as quickly as possible."

What Hank tells me is not really new to me. I'm aware that this often happens. Although I have to admit that when I hear it from the customer's perspective, I understand why it sucks.

Before I can respond, Hank continues: "And that's not all, Ronnie. After three months of waiting, they came to install the kitchen. After a day of working, the kitchen was assembled. But nothing worked: water and electricity were not connected at all! Our representative said casually that his job was done. The salesman appeared to have forgotten to include this in the contract. After a phone call to the planning department, it turned out that they had to wait another two weeks for an engineer to come over and finish the job. Isn't it terrible? In the end, my friends moved into their new home much later than planned. He is now teasing me all the time with 'Kitchen Slow' instead of Kitchen Quick! This is total bullcrap! How much time does it really take to install a kitchen? Three days?!? And they had to wait more than three months?!? We should be able to do this much faster, shouldn't we, Ronnie?"

I feel attacked and I become defensive: "Listen, Hank, the placement only takes a few days. But there is a lot more work involved than just that. The room needs to be measured, and the kitchen needs to be produced. We have to order all kitchen equipment, and that often includes a delivery time. Moreover, your friend is not our only customer. A lot of kitchens are being sold, so he will just have to wait for his turn."

Hank responds fiercely: "Bullshit! Why can't we do it faster? This is bad advertising!" I think about whether I should start talking about the time when Hank was managing director. In those days the delivery time wasn't any better. In fact, it was much more unpredictable. Sometimes they delivered in six weeks, but there were also periods with a delivery time of almost half a year. Anyway, I've brought it up before, but I never win the argument. He always has good reasons why it was different back then and why it is possible now. I just let it go. Ultimately, the company is doing very well financially. And taking some occasional hits from Hank is part of my job.

Like most work days, the rest of the day is filled with a meeting marathon. Apart from the morning session, I hardly ever have time to talk to my colleagues spontaneously. After the meetings, I need at least another hour or two to respond to email: I receive at least two hundred emails every day. Sometimes it seems endless and I wonder how I could improve this.

In the afternoon I have a meeting with a possible new supplier. A new player in the market, specialized in plastic kitchen tops. I have a nice conversation with the salesman and I promise that we will certainly do business. He invites me to have dinner with their CEO soon. I gladly accept his offer: I love good food.

In the evening I have a business appointment in a stylish restaurant. At my previous employer, the supermarket chain, we worked a lot with consulting firms. Even though I no longer work there, they like to keep in touch. They often send me invitations for speeches or roundtable sessions. Tonight there is a CEO dinner. I really enjoy learning from my fellow directors.

When I walk into the living room at 10:30 p.m., Emily is already sleeping on the couch. She is holding a book: *The Power of Self-Management*. This may be an interesting book for me to read after she is finished. I carefully grab the book from her hands and put it away. I cover her with a blanket, turn off the light, and walk up the stairs to our bedroom. When I wake up the next morning, she lies in bed next to me. I didn't notice she sneaked in.

⌀

The weeks and days fly by. Every day looks similar to the other. Everything is steady and under control.

I had no idea this was the proverbial calm before the storm.

Toast

Four weeks later, Friday evening at 8:00 p.m.

I climb on my chair. I tap my champagne glass and shout: "Hello, everyone! Can I have your attention for a moment please?" The room is chock-full of people. My people. Our people. They are all hard-working craftsmen. After I repeat myself a few times, it becomes silent. Everyone looks in my direction. I say: "I want to make a toast."

The whole week we were working against a very tough deadline. It got me constantly anxious about whether we would get the job done on time. I pushed my people a lot and made sure they continued working over the weekends and at night. That didn't make me popular. Maybe I misused my power a bit too much. But I had to do it—I was cornered.

A few times a day Hank called me for an update. Most of the time I couldn't tell him if we would make it. For a long while, it didn't look good. But this morning I was able to report for the first time that we would probably make it right on time. And we did. At exactly 6:00 p.m., we were finished and I could give Hank the redeeming phone call. It worked! He was relieved and said: "Go and celebrate it tonight with everyone who helped. Money is not an issue; I will pay!" Although I don't normally like to spend a lot of money, he didn't have to say that twice. This was indeed an opportunity to celebrate. I immediately called a very good restaurant in the area and reserved a room there for an extended dinner with everyone who had helped. I also asked my entire management team to join. We needed this success.

I continue my speech: "I am extremely proud of all your hard work. It was only two weeks ago that Hank called me and said 'Ronald, the crown princess is going to move into a student house. Well, actually, she is moving into her own apartment in a separate wing of the royal palace. They need to renovate it first, and we have a good chance to be able to supply the kitchen!' That is pretty cool, of course. These kinds of assignments are very rare. Who is able to get into the royal palace anyway? But, of course, you know Hank: he sometimes presents a new customer lead as if it is already a certainty, so I want to especially thank our 'Mr. Teflon,' who actually closed the deal. Paul, thank you so much! However, when you afterward told me we had to deliver within two weeks, I thought you had gone crazy. Two weeks!! Delivering such a large kitchen within fourteen days? That seemed crazy to me. But the deal was closed; we couldn't go back anymore. It seemed like an impossible task, but we succeeded! Thanks to you. Thanks to all of you! But let's not only toast to ourselves, but also to all other colleagues on the production floor and in the office. These colleagues also had to go the extra mile to handle all the other customers. They may not be here tonight, but we would never have succeeded without them. So thank you all again. The crown princess from now on cooks in her Kitchen Quick Kitchen! Isn't that amazing?!?"

From the back of the room, Laura's charming voice sounds: "Yeah right! Do you really think she cooks herself?" The room fills with laughter.

I raise my glass and say: "Cheers, everyone! Kudos to you, and enjoy the food!" The glasses clink. I climb off the chair and sit down at the table that is reserved for my management team.

Laura, the customer service manager, sits down to my left. She turns towards me, looks at me incisively through her black glasses, and says: "Hey, Ronald, this is all nice, but do you realize that the telephones are red-hot with angry customers? We have indeed made the princess happy, but all deliveries to quite a large number of other customers have been postponed for at least two weeks."

Paul, the sales and planning director, responds before I can. He says: "F*ck the other customers, Laura! Do you know how much money we have earned with this? And think of the halo effect: I can now tell everyone everywhere that we are a supplier of the royal family. Count the money!"

Laura reacts angrily: "They are also your customers, Paul!" But then again, your job is easy. You just have to close the deal and then you throw it over the fence. The rest of the company has to handle it further, while you are counting your bonus money."

In the meantime, I have been able to think and say: "You are right, Laura, but we are all going to smooth it out. Let's celebrate tonight! This is really an exceptional situation. Call it force majeure. And we made it happen! Come and top up my glass!"

After my third glass of champagne, I decide that I can no longer drive home. I text Emily that I'm going to stay at a hotel. She reacts immediately and tells me that she had not expected anything else.

The party goes on for a long time. I get back to my hotel at 1:30 a.m. And that night, I sleep like a baby.

Formula Kitchen

Halfway through May, Sunday afternoon at 1:00 p.m.

Time flew quickly after the night we celebrated installing the princess's kitchen. This success kept us motivated, giving us the momentum to complete our backlog. Everything is back to normal again. The usual day-to-day business determines your agenda and before you know it, another week has passed.

Sunday afternoon is me-time. Relaxing in front of the TV while clearing my head. Usually, I watch sports: football, ice hockey, car racing—it doesn't really matter, as long as I don't have to think about it too much. I lie down on the couch and put the pillows under my head. Emily smiles at me and says, "Are you ready for your Sunday afternoon nap?" She is right. I often fall asleep while watching. Especially when watching Formula One racing. The start is always very spectacular and, of course, the pit stops as well. But if the race is not too exciting, I usually close my eyes for a while. Isn't that nice?

This weekend it's time for the Spanish Grand Prix. Emily sits down on the couch next to me. "I really don't understand what you like about it," she notes. "Car racing is so boring! They drive a few hundred kilometers and then they are in exactly the same place again. Along the way, little happens, but they do blow tons of CO_2 into the atmosphere. Moreover, the same drivers always finish on the podium."

I respond: "Oh well, if you look at it more often it will actually become more interesting. Don't we also watch TV series? In many episodes, nothing really happens. But because you know the characters and storylines, it is still enjoyable to watch. Formula 1 is similar to a TV-series. Every race is a new episode. Anyway, I'm going to get back to watching, the pre-race broadcast is starting!" Emily shrugs her shoulders, picks up a study book and starts browsing.

An energetic conversation is taking place in the TV studio. I'm impressed by how much these guys know about car racing and the amount of details that are part of the sport. Fortunately, it is not all too serious and there is also plenty of laughter in the studio. I enjoy it the most when they switch live to the circuit. As always, there is enough to report. From Spain, the commentator explains which innovations the teams have implemented since the last race. They are usually very small improvements, but these tweaks have compounding benefits throughout the season. Despite the enormous speeds of these cars, the difference is still in hundredths of a second. Pretty bizarre if you think about it.

The race is about to start. One more long commercial break before it begins. I walk to the kitchen to grab a bottle of beer. When I return to the room, I recognize the jingle of our own TV commercial. I respond enthusiastically: "Cool! Our ad made it as a Formula 1 commercial." I lump down on the couch and look at the screen.

I immediately notice that it is a completely different commercial than our usual one. Emily says: "Hey, did you have the ad changed?" I am astonished because I wasn't informed about this. I grab the remote control and turn up the volume. As always, Hank plays the lead role. But this time he wears racing overalls and the usual cowboy hat, but without the scantily clad models by his side.

I hear Hank say: "The new standard: Formula-Kitchen. Order today, and it will be installed within two weeks. If not, you will get the kitchen for free! Get it on time or you won't pay a dime!" Then he gets into a racing car and drives away from the camera with a lot of noise. For several seconds, the screen keeps showing: "Formula Kitchen: placing kitchens like a pit stop!" while the voice-over repeats that you don't have to pay if we don't deliver within two weeks.

Did I hear it correctly? Supplying and installing a kitchen within fourteen days? And if it doesn't work, then customers will get their money back!? It is slowly sinking in. How could he! This is impossible! I say to Emily: "He really went crazy. This is not possible at all!" I don't wait for her reply and I grab my phone from my pocket to call Hank. I get his voicemail. With his American accent he sounds enthusiastic: "Heeeeeey, this is Hank Rapid. Speak your message after the beep!" I say: "Hank, what the f*ck?! Why did you launch this new ad? This can't be true. It is impossible! And you don't have to pay if we don't deliver? Where did you get this ridiculous idea? Please call me back!"

I pace back and forth. My mind is racing. I think out loud: "Where did he get this idea? We were able to install a kitchen with the crown princess in two weeks. But that was an exception! Everything had to be put aside for that. And now he wants us to do this for all customers? Impossible! And then also the guarantee that if we don't deliver on time they don't have to pay? Hank has gone crazy!"

I say in frustration: "Emily, how the hell am I going to solve this? It would be better if Hank would really retire, once and for all. He has mentioned many times that he wants our company to become faster, but forcing it this way is uncalled for!"

Emily tries to calm me down: "Chill out, Ronald. I'm sure it will be alright. Don't overreact. It is his business; he owns all the risk. It is his money, right? After all, you always say that the company is his pension. Give the guy a break. If he wants to throw away his fortune this way, then it is his choice!"

After a few seconds of silence, she adds: "And on the sunny side, if the company goes out of business, we're relieved of those annoying commercials!"

I respond: "The company going out of business? I won't let that happen. I won't let all my colleagues and their families be affected by this!"

Frustrated, I walk out the door. I don't care at all anymore about the race. I have to go outside. "I'm going to ride my bike," I tell Emily.

She responds calmly: "I understand, honey. Clear your head."

I take my bike out of the shed and ride onto the street. I've never pedaled so hard in my life. So much on my mind. I hardly feel my legs.

Interview

After two hours of biking, my anger has completely cooled down. Emily is actually right: it is Hank's company. So what am I worried about? He runs a greater risk than me... And in hindsight: in all our previous commercials he also promised a faster delivery time than we could ever deliver. So in that way, nothing has really changed.

After I take a shower, I receive a call from an unknown number. A cheerful female voice sounds: "Hey. Hello, Ronald. This is Shirley from BBC's *The One Show*. You are the managing director of Kitchen Quick, correct?"

I reply hesitantly: "Yes, that's me. What can I do for you?"

Shirley responds immediately: "Well, on our special weekend edition we always have an item about entrepreneurs. We'd love to hear more about your campaign of offering an installed kitchen within fourteen days. I'm particularly curious about the promise that if you don't succeed, you don't have to pay. Our editor-in-chief was watching Formula 1 this afternoon and he saw your new commercial. We couldn't catch Hank the Kitchen Cowboy himself, so that's why I'm calling you. Do you want to be in the broadcast tonight?"

I have no desire at all to say yes to her. After all, I don't understand this idiotic idea either. Let alone explain it on television. But all of a sudden I have an epiphany. Maybe if I go, I'm able to spin the story. For example, I could say that it only applies to standard kitchens that we can supply from stock. Or maybe I can even say that it is a temporary promotion, only for the first twenty customers, for example. "Okay fine!" I hear myself answer, to my own surprise.

"Perfect," Shirley replies. "We will see you tonight at the studio in London just before 7:00 p.m. I'll send you the address in the meantime."

I wonder if I just made a brilliant move or made a huge mistake. I walk into my home office and try to think logically and prepare. What should I say and not say tonight? How are we going to solve this in our company? The most sensible thing to say is that it is true, but it is limited to this month and, of course, only applies to standard kitchens. We probably won't get away with that, but then the possible refunds from customers are still manageable. Moreover, we can perhaps add some small print so that we do not have to pay back at all. I try to call Hank a number of times, but I keep getting his voicemail. Emily brings me something to eat. I can tell by the way she looks that she feels bad for me.

✍

I drive away from home on time. As soon as I am on the road for half an hour, my phone rings. I recognize Shirley's number from BBC: "Hi, Ronald... Oh, I can hear you are already in the car? Sorry I'm doing this so last minute, but I'm calling to cancel it tonight. We managed to get Hank himself after all. So we decided to put him on TV. Actually, he's already here. Thank you for your effort, I hope you don't mind!" Before I can reply, she hangs up.

Well, damn it! I exit the highway and turn around immediately. Once I'm home, Emily is already sitting on the couch with the television on, ready to watch the item with me in the studio. She is stunned that I'm back. I explain that Hank is in the studio himself. She says: "Oh no, what mischief! But nothing you can do about it. Come here. Sit down next to me. It's starting now." The opening tune of the program sounds through the speakers.

The camera zooms in on a desk. Hank is standing behind it in his racing overalls and cowboy hat. Of course. The presenter says: "Today we have in our studio Hank Rapid, entrepreneur and founder of Kitchen Quick. Hank, Welcome!"

Hank answers cheerfully and with a big smile: "Thanks for having me! It's a pleasure to be here!"

The presenter continues: "Great! We'd like to scrutinize something. You recently announced the policy that kitchens are installed within two weeks; otherwise, you get your money back. This is unique in the market, and even impossible according to your competitors. Is it really true? Or is this yet another misleading sales trick that kitchen vendors are famous for?"

Hank doesn't respond to the hateful comment and proudly says: "No, not at all. It is actually very simple. We recently placed a kitchen in the Queen's Palace. And super fast, within two weeks. Hence our new policy. If it is possible for the Queen's daughter, then it must be possible for everyone. Every customer deserves a royal treatment! After all, the customer is king..." He looks into the camera with a big grin.

I listen with astonishment to everything Hank has to say. He confirms that it's really true. Delivery within fourteen days; otherwise, no payment. And it applies to all kitchens. When the presenter digs deeper and suggests that it's probably a temporary offer, Hank responds firmly: "No, this is not temporary! We are going to do this, definitive and forever. There is no small print!"

It sinks in that we won't be able to bail out of it. This is serious. We have to get to work.

I quickly send two texts to my entire management team. The first one is: "Have you seen BBC One tonight? Hank was on *The One Show*. You won't believe what he said. Watch the replay. He's at the beginning of the show..."

I immediately add: "Tomorrow, extra meeting!! At 10:00 a.m. in the large meeting room. Please clear your schedule."

That night it takes a long time before I'm able to fall asleep. There is one question that keeps racing through my head: how the hell am I going to solve this?

PART TWO

Qualifying

Deliberation

Monday morning – average delivery time: twelve weeks

The next day, I arrive early to the office. Despite the restless night, I feel strong. Somehow this challenge energizes me. When I turn onto the parking lot at 6:15 a.m., I am not the first one there. I see Laura and Paul's cars. I assume they are already busy considering different scenarios. Paul must be looking at the planning. And Laura is probably adjusting the call scripts and crunching the numbers from a customer perspective.

When I walk into the office, I first get myself a double espresso. When I let the first warm sips slip in, I feel the caffeine entering my bloodstream immediately. Delicious! I walk to my office and close the door. I need to prepare for the meeting. I really want to make sure that we tackle this problem as a team.

At exactly 10:00 a.m., I enter the large meeting room. Typically our meetings start five to ten minutes later because people arrive late, but I am pleasantly surprised to see my entire management team on time.

The atmosphere is tense. Laura's face looks worried, and Wilma, who is responsible for the Placement department, sits with her arms crossed. Wilma is always very precise— kitchens must be installed airtight and level. "Quality takes time," she always says. This new situation probably makes her very anxious.

I sit down and start: "Thank you all for clearing your schedules for this emergency meeting." Laura takes a deep breath and looks at me angrily. I continue, undisturbed: "You all watched the TV show last night, I suppose? Just like you, I knew nothing about it. Unfortunately, I haven't managed to get in touch with Hank yet, but when I do, I will demand an explanation. I'm just as upset about it as you are. I don't think we'll get away with it. We will have to look for a way to considerably shorten our delivery time."

Thom "The Saw" is the first to say something: "Ronald, don't worry so much. This is probably one of Hank's trial balloons again. It is obviously unrealistic, like most of his ideas. In a few weeks, he will realize that it is not feasible and he will reverse his decision."

Laura responds: "I don't know, Thom. I think it is the first time that he has made such an idea publicly known. On television. In an advertising campaign. And even on BBC! I don't see him reeling back so quickly. Think about how humiliating that would be for him."

Thom responds again: "Calm down, everyone. I have been working here for so many years, and it is always the same story. It all starts with a lot of fanfare and good plans, but it won't lead anywhere. So don't worry. This will blow over again. Moreover, a kitchen installed that fast, is that even necessary? Is there a customer that really wants this? What nonsense!"

But Paul definitely does not agree with that at all. He slams the table with a flat hand: "Customers love it! We have only been open for an hour, and people are queuing at our showrooms to order their kitchens. I think you are all very negative. I believe this is great!! Normally, May is a terrible month. But if it continues like this, it may become the best month ever."

He continues cheerfully: "Hank really shows his entrepreneurship. Doing something that all competitors consider impossible. Amazing! Nothing is impossible!! Hank is shaking up the entire market, and we have the opportunity to become a market leader. We have never managed such an influx of new customers. I'm really looking forward to it!"

At that point, Laura can no longer restrain herself. "That's easy for you to say, Paul. You only have to close the deals. After that, you don't need to look back anymore. But to be clear: a signed deal is only the beginning! Then the rest of us have to work hard to make it happen. I arrived extra early because I saw the troubles coming. And like I expected, the phones have been red hot at our customer service since 9:00 a.m. But not with people ordering. Instead, we have dozens of customers calling that have been waiting for their kitchens for weeks and are now claiming a free kitchen!! Do you think this will blow over? Come and answer a few phone calls in my department. That will change your mind!"

I interrupt the discussion: "Take it easy! There is no reason to argue with each other about this. We are a team, so we have to solve this together. By the way, I think Laura is right. We must bear in mind that we will not get this reversed. Hank will probably still overrule us, even if we all disagree with him. You heard from Laura and Paul that our customers take it very seriously. So we should do that too. Let's try to make the best of it. So stop bickering. What should we do now? Any ideas?"

Paul opens his laptop and shows us a graph: "I just looked at the data. We need way more capacity. The delivery time of a kitchen is now, on average, twelve weeks. We will never reduce that without extra capacity. Therefore, I propose that we temporarily cancel all holidays and days off and ask people to continue working in the evenings and over the weekend. I also recommend that you hire ten extra temps from the employment agency."

Thom responds: "Yes, that makes sense. We have been too busy for far too long. And adding extra hands to my department is a good idea anyway. It is smart to expand production if this will lead to more orders." Thom then turns to Laura and says: "The peak in customer calls is temporary; you understand that, right? Just let your people work overtime for a few days. No one has ever died of working too hard."

Laura responds fiercely: "Yeah right! We can't work overtime all the time, can we? The workload is already very high. If we continue like this, people will get burned out." I think about what she says. The customer service people have indeed been very busy for a long time. Because we often deliver later than we promise, they receive many complaints and often have to handle difficult telephone calls.

Paul says: "Well, on the other hand, we employ quite a few unmotivated people who could use a kick in the ass. If you can't handle a little extra work, then you're simply not fit to work here." I'm quite shocked by what Paul says. Do we employ unmotivated people? Why are our people unmotivated? I make a note to circle back to Paul later.

Laura is getting even angrier now. Her face turns red. She swallows her words, and the only thing that comes out of her mouth is "Pffffff." During the rest of the meeting, she doesn't say a word.

"Calm down, everyone," I intervene. "I understand that you are frustrated about the situation, but we have to keep cool and work together. Arranging more capacity in the short term is a good idea; let's do that. But we not only have to work harder, but also smarter. Are there any other quick wins?"

Thom responds: "Yes, certainly. If we are going to receive more orders, we must now order more materials. We shouldn't wait until our stock suddenly runs out, stopping our production. So, we should fill-up the warehouse now with sheet material. I will immediately place an order with our suppliers. There is plenty of space, so that is a quick win!" He then looks at Wilma and says: "What do you want? What do you think? You haven't said anything yet."

This is a recurring pattern in my management team. Thom, the production manager, and Wilma, the placement manager, are opposites. That in itself is not bad in a team like mine, but Wilma often remains quiet when others speak up. Thom always knows immediately what is needed, while Wilma is more thoughtful and needs a little more time. By the time Wilma has a proposal, the rest is already one step ahead. And that's a shame because her ideas are often very good. She often comes up with things we haven't thought of.

Wilma replies: "I do see this as an opportunity to improve things a lot, but I think it is important that we keep the quality at a high level. In terms of quick wins, I don't have anything right now, but I think if I ask my people, they will come up with ideas. They do the actual placement work with the customers, so they know best. I think we should ask them where we could improve. Perhaps it would be even better to do a full-company offsite to think this through. We are not smarter than our people who actually do the work!"

Thom shakes his head and says: "What a weak idea! Offsites are a waste of time. We'll leave the offsite with good intentions and vague action plans that never get implemented. And we will waste precious hours people could use to get work done. And at the end of the day, they will still look to us for the solution. No, we just have to tighten control. I intend to pay closer attention to my people, as we can no longer afford mistakes. Our relaxed and laissez-faire workplace needs to change. We should stop talking and start working!" Wilma remains silent and stares at the table.

I take a moment to think about what Thom just said. He is right, we should control things a little more tightly, but it doesn't really feel like it is a solution to micromanage our people. That won't accomplish anything. They are already working very hard. Wilma's proposal to involve our people appeals to me. Maybe we shouldn't close down the whole company for an offsite. But it is smart to ask our people for proposals.

Wilma gathers her thoughts and turns to Thom. "Thom, I would like to sit down with you soon to see if we can achieve some improvements in the process between our departments."

Thom opens his laptop and scrolls through his meeting schedule: "Sure, just schedule a meeting and we'll talk about it. But keep in mind that I already have a packed agenda in the coming weeks."

I notice we're not making any progress. And we really have to do something to solve this crisis. I think back to how we solved things like this in my previous job at the supermarket chain. I suddenly remember what our CFO always said: if you can't measure it, it doesn't exist.

I say with determination: "Okay, everyone, we are all busy, so I would like to conclude the meeting. First of all, let's immediately implement the quick wins that we see ourselves. Additionally, let's keep our heads cool and try to comprehend the current situation before we suddenly start changing things."

"Paul, can you at least ask your colleagues in the planning department to measure the delivery time of each kitchen? We should make a distinction between kitchens that we have already sold and are now going to sell using the new formula." Paul nods. I continue: "And please don't start selling like crazy. We're not ready for it yet. Tell your salespeople that they can schedule appointments with new customers, but try to schedule them as ahead of time as possible. This gives the rest of us time to get things sorted." Paul nods affirmatively, but I instinctively feel that he will probably ignore my instruction. After all, he has the opportunity to increase his annual bonus considerably this month if he scores some extra orders. I make a mental note for myself to call him about this in the afternoon.

I tell Laura: "Laura, this campaign does not apply to customers who have already ordered. You should be clear about that when they call. It only applies to new orders!" Laura doesn't respond; she is still angry.

I conclude with: "I also think we need external help. From my previous job, I know a consultancy agency full of folks who have dealt with situations like this. I'm going to ask them to come and help us." The team responds positively. I think they are relieved that I take charge.

✕

After the meeting, I immediately call Pamela from the Full Control Consulting Group (FCCG in short). I remember her from my previous job. She has since been promoted from senior manager to partner. I explain the problem to her, and she immediately gives me the feeling that she can help me. For the first time, it feels like I'm not on my own. In our conversation, she asks me if I have ever heard of TEM—Total Efficiency Management. It appears to be a proven method with which you can accelerate processes in a measured way. That sounds good! I schedule an appointment with her for later in the week and ask her if she could immediately send us a quote. After all, we have to make progress quickly.

Nothing Is Impossible

That evening I finally get in touch with Hank. It's a tough conversation. I always find it very difficult to discuss issues with Hank because he's strong at articulating and defending his point of view. He also doesn't hesitate to make it personal.

He dismisses my objections. It has been a thorn in his side for years that things are going so slowly. Moreover, Hank was in China last month. And it has become clear to him that a wave of cheap kitchens will soon flood the market. He wants to be ahead of that development. He doesn't really want to compete on price, but he thinks we can on speed.

For too long, he accepted all arguments that it couldn't be done. He has now discovered it was all unfounded. His main reasoning is: if it is possible for the crown princess, then it must be possible for all customers!

I tried to counter that by saying that the crown princess' kitchen was an exception and very difficult to repeat. But Hank puts that aside quite easily with the argument that it was the largest kitchen we've ever built. So for other customers, it should be even faster! He completely ignores my objection that her kitchen was built at the expense of other customers.

When Hank says that a real managing director sees nothing as impossible, I budge. He is clearly determined to continue with this. He ends with "Make it happen, Ronnie. I have confidence in you!"

I immediately ask him for a budget to hire FCCG. Needless to say, FCCG consultants aren't inexpensive. Fortunately enough that was no problem at all. He said that this is the time to fix it once and for all. He would fully bear the resulting losses. He had put aside plenty of money for that. Hank spoke the legendary words: "Whatever you need, Ronnie! Money is no issue; I have very deep pockets!" Perhaps I should have asked how deep exactly.

The rest of the month the company is in survival mode. Everyone runs from one place to another and really tries their best. I am proud to see what we can achieve if everyone puts their best foot forward. At the same time, I realize that Laura is right: we cannot sustain this pace for very long.

Nightmare

A month later, mid-June – the
average delivery time has risen
from twelve to sixteen weeks

Complaints are pouring in. The additional orders have created a logistical nightmare. Although Paul says that he has done his utmost to curb his sellers, we have sold far more kitchens than usual. It looks like the entire company has ground to a halt because of the extra orders. I even understood we placed the wrong kitchen at two customers' houses last week. That has never happened to us in all of our existence.

There seems to be another problem. To reduce our delivery time and prevent us from having to give kitchens away for free, we let new customers take priority over old ones. Even though they were already scheduled, we forgot to deliver the kitchens to a lot of our older customers. What's more, the planning department forgot to inform these customers that their kitchens were coming later than promised. Despite the extra people and all the extra efforts of everyone, the situation has become much worse. Our data shows that the average delivery time is only increasing.

The editorial offices of investigative TV programs are constantly on the phone. Every day, I have an invitation to appear on television. In the meantime, Hank is nowhere to be seen. When there is positive news, he'll gladly sit on TV with his sun-tanned head, but now that everything is a mess, he doesn't show up.

After insisting for a long time, I was able to convince Hank to stop the advertising campaign for the time being. Finally, a win. At first, he didn't want to hear about it. After all, it led to quite a lot of new orders. And because he only was in touch with "Mr. Teflon," he wasn't aware of all the problems. "Everything is going well, Ronnie!" he tried to make clear to me. "We have never sold this much!"

Only after I sent him the figures with the increasing delivery time and the enormous growth in customer complaints, he caved in. He allowed for some time for us to recover and until then, he wouldn't show the TV ads for Formula Kitchen. This disappointed Emily, as the original ad (with Hank and two half-naked models) is back on air. In the meantime, the Formula Kitchen offer remains in effect, but only for customers who explicitly ask for it.

Fortunately, the team of FCCG consultants was able to start very quickly. It was very impressive. From day one they immediately arrived with a team of six people. They're all very professional. All dressed very well in suits and ties. All highly educated and really smart. But I do wonder to what extent they understand what we're doing here: most of them are so young that I think they have never bought a kitchen themselves.

So far I have only spoken to Pamela on the phone. But that would change soon, she promised me.

Improved Steering

Friday morning

Today FCCG is going to present their findings and acceleration plan to our management team. Although the location is not very inspiring—a musty hotel and conference center close to the highway—I'm looking forward to it.

It wasn't easy to persuade Thom "The Saw" to go off-site for a day, but when I drive into the parking lot, I'm relieved I see him getting out of his car. He drives a small family car, which barely fits his huge body. "Mornin, boss" he greets me, while we walk together to the entrance of the hotel. An electronic sign in the lobby reads "Kitchen Quick–meeting room F1." A friendly receptionist tells us that we have to go up the stairs to the first floor. I was here a few years ago when it was already faded glory. It hasn't gotten much better since.

In the hallway, Thom and I follow the signs, A1, B1, up to F1. Here it is. We are the first to arrive. Everything is neatly prepared. A long U-shaped table fills the space. A projector stands on top of it, facing a huge screen on the wall. In the corner of the room there is a table with coffee and teapots and bottles of soda. I pour a cup of coffee, take a sip, and spit it out almost immediately. "Blegh!" I say aloud.

Thom looks at me questioningly. "I think they have warmed up yesterday's coffee in a microwave." I quickly slide in a cookie to get rid of the taste.

My colleagues arrive one by one. Laura, Wilma, and then Paul too. Exactly at 10:00 a.m., at the agreed time, Pamela comes in with a colleague. "Ronald!" she shouts very energetically, spreading her arms and giving me a hug. I have always found Pamela an impressive woman. She has long dark brown hair, dark eyes, and a charming smile. She is very hard working, from early in the morning until late at night. Not the type that can sit and relax on the couch. Pamela always carries a trolley suitcase with all the files of all her projects. Whenever she is around, I'm a bit on my guard. She can be very temperamental and intense.

Pamela connects her small laptop to the projector and starts her presentation. "Look, that kitchen factory of yours, you can compare it with a complicated, unclear traffic situation," she says with her Italian accent. She shows a colorful photo of a three-lane roundabout with six different turns, with cycle paths through it. She continues: "This roundabout is very complicated and unclear. Therefore, the people on the roundabout will hesitate and brake at unexpected moments. This blocks traffic flow. But can you blame the people for that?" She stays silent for a moment.

After a few seconds, Laura responds: "No, of course not. The person who designed the roundabout is an amateur!"

Pamela continues: "Exactly, you simply cannot expect people to know how to use this roundabout properly. In other words: everyone is doing their own thing. When people act on their own judgment, you have no control over the process and you cannot predict what will happen. To solve this, you have to give people better instructions." Before anyone can ask a question, she moves on to the next slide. "Improved steering is actually easy to achieve. If you put traffic controllers in the right places, who tell the cars exactly when they can enter the roundabout or when to wait, it will be resolved in no time.

57

And for cyclists, there will be traffic lights and crossings. It has to be safe, you know."

Yes, this sounds logical to me. I look at the faces of my colleagues, who also nod in agreement. Thom, in particular, seems very enthusiastic.

Pamela continues: "You can do the same for companies: making sure employees do the right things at the right time. Ensuring there will be no traffic jams in the work. We call this Total Efficiency Management. It is the name of the method we use to implement this at organizations such as yours."

Pamela's story lands well with the entire management team. Except for Laura. A frown is visible behind her glasses. She raises her hand: "But isn't that exactly what they do in the planning department? What is so new and special about this?" Paul, who is the manager of planning, is clearly impressed by Laura's question and is all ears.

Pamela responds in agreement: "That's right; you prepare a detailed schedule for each day. But with Total Efficiency Management, you also add process coordinators who are continuously making operational decisions about what needs to be done and when. They're like real-time, end-to-end traffic controllers. Look, your plans are fine. But a plan is no more than a plan. It's just a static document. It's the implementation that counts. The action that results from it. That is why the process coordinators will ensure that everything actually goes according to plan!" Laura and Paul seem convinced that it will help to actually implement the plans.

Pamela moves to the next slide, which also looks professional. "We interviewed several of your people last week to chart the current process. We have also measured the time within the process, and I must say I have good news! The improvement potential is really huge!" The slide contains an impressive table full of numbers, including the efficiency per department. Paul immediately notes that his department scores best.

"We are convinced that we can improve efficiency by at least a factor of twenty. And that's exactly what you need to reduce the delivery time to less than two weeks." A picture appears on the projector with a line graph showing how, within a few weeks, the delivery time will be reduced to two weeks.

This sounds and looks great. It's almost too good to be true. The underlying statistics and analysis are very convincing. I'm glad I brought in FCCG. Smart advisors often see and know things that you can't think of yourself. If what Pamela says is true, then we are quickly back in control. I now understand why they are called the Full Control Consultancy Group...

Yet I still have a strange feeling. I have learned from my grandfather that when something seems too good to be true, it often is. Therefore I ask critically: "How are you going to measure whether it works, Pamela? And what does your planning look like?"

"I was just going to a slide that touches on that, Ronald," says Pamela. "You are just one step ahead of me! This slide shows an example of the management report that we'll deliver on a weekly basis. You will always find the latest metrics on it, such as the lead time of each kitchen. First, you see the total, then you can drill down to each process step. We'll also show the RAG status for a number of critical performance indicators. such as quality and efficiency."

"RAG status?" says Thom. Pamela looks at Thom for a moment but doesn't seem to understand why he is asking this question. She also scans the room to see if more people don't know what that means.

She is clearly surprised that it turns out not to be a well-known term: "Yes, RAG. Red, amber, green. If everything is green, everything is going according to plan. If it's red, it is going terribly. And if it's amber, you have to start paying attention."

Thom replies: "Ah, you are going to install traffic lights. You could have just said so!"

Pamela continues, undisturbed, with her presentation. It seems that she really has thought of everything. Her step-by-step plan and timetable look very sleek and professional. Then she looks at me and says: "To answer your other question, Ronald: as far as I'm concerned, we can start the implementation immediately. And if we can move full steam ahead, it can be completed within four weeks. Provided you decide today and we start immediately on Monday."

"Only four weeks? That sounds good," I say. "What are the first steps?"

ℬ

In the hours that follow, we go over the implementation plan. We discuss the new way of working of each department, based on a detailed handbook that FCCG has prepared. Process steps, roles, responsibilities, and metrics are clearly described. Pamela's colleague, a young twenty-something-year-old, processes all comments and remarks in the handbook immediately. We can watch the changes being made on the screen. There is a positive atmosphere, where we as a management team are really analyzing and solving the problem together. I think it is the first time that people listen to each other and think as a team.

"But, Pamela, how can we ensure people actually change their behavior?" Thom asks.

Pamela answers: "Good question. We sometimes see other customers adding a KPI to the annual performance review cycle, whereby you make it compulsory for every employee to write a development agreement about working more efficiently. That way you can really guarantee the change. It then becomes a goal of everyone personally." Pamela looks at her young colleague and says, "Can you add it to the handbook, Conner?" Conner nods and types eagerly on his laptop.

✍

At the end of the afternoon, we are ready. It feels like we are close to solving the problem. The gut feeling I had is not completely gone yet, but I think that this is our best chance to improve.

"I think the job is done. Well done, team! It is now simply a matter of rolling out the change. Does anyone have any doubts?" I ask.

I look at everyone one by one. Paul and Thom react enthusiastically and almost say in unison: "No!" Wilma and Laura seem a little more reserved but show no doubts by shaking their heads lightly. Something in me says that that means they are not fully on board yet, but if they don't agree, this is the moment they should say something.

I wait a moment and then say: "Okay then, we all agree. I will now send the announcement." I open my laptop and type the following email:

```
From: Ronald
To: Everyone
Subject: Accelerator program

Hello all,
```

Today we had a strategy day with the management team and we decided to implement Total Efficiency Management immediately. This is a proven method that does exactly what we need: speeding up our processes. In view of the new Formula Kitchen proposition, we must take immediate action.

Please read the enclosed slides and the new process manual carefully, as the implementation by FCCG will start next Monday.

If there are any questions, please let me or your supervisor know. They are fully informed and support this initiative.

Kind regards,

Ronald

Like snow melting under the sun, our problems disappeared over the next four weeks. The delivery time quickly reduced to just one week!

At least, that's what I dreamt of. In reality, it was a complete disaster.

Ultimatum

Hank unexpectedly enters my office and sits down next to me. He puts a hand on my shoulder insistently. "Ronnie, how is it going?"

"Oh hi, Hank. Did we have a meeting scheduled? Well, it doesn't matter, I have some time now. How are you? I will show you our progress." I open the management report on my laptop, showing the traffic lights and I say proudly: "The implementation of Total Efficiency Management is going well." He doesn't look at the screen, but keeps staring at me "Total...what?"

I respond: "Total Efficiency Management, our new way of working! The delivery time has already improved considerably, but we are not quite there yet. With help from FCCG, we have identified a few major bottlenecks in the process. I will share an example. As you know, the Placement department was always responsible for ordering the kitchen equipment and that resulted in added delivery time. Before a kitchen could be installed, we had to wait for a few weeks for the equipment to arrive. But from now on, we'll order the equipment immediately after the order has been placed, so we'll never have to wait again. A nice quick win. And that's just the beginning. We have gone from sixteen weeks to an average of ten weeks. An improvement of 60 percent!"

Hank gets up promptly and starts pacing the room. He remains silent for a few seconds but then starts yelling: "This cannot be true! It has been over three months since the new commercial, and you have managed to shorten the delivery time from twelve to ten weeks?! Do you have any idea what this costs?"

I look at him perplexed and realize that if you put it that way, it doesn't sound good. Hank continues: "By the way, I spoke to Paul for a moment and discovered that the biggest reason for your shorter delivery time is something completely different."

"Because all the old customers started to receive their kitchens later, many of them withdrew their orders. That is what you see in your statistics. No improved delivery times. But canceled orders. That's what you see! Damn lies those statistics!"

I feel the rug pulled out from underneath me. How can Hank know better, while he is hardly involved? How is it possible that the numbers are incorrect? Why didn't Paul inform me?

Hank urgently asks me: "Ronnie, when did you last talk to a customer?"

For a moment, I hesitate. I sincerely couldn't remember when the last time was. I reply hesitantly: "Uhm, that was about a month or two ago, I guess."

Hank's question makes me think. The implementation by FCCG required much more of my time than I expected. In particular, the number of escalations that I need to handle has increased enormously. As a result, I am in meetings more often than I would like. All the other work continues as usual, which means that I work many more evenings than before. Emily regularly makes comments about the fact that I am at home a lot less. Even though she is busy with her studies and her work, she is increasingly home alone. I assume this is the reason why she starts talking about becoming pregnant and that she needs me home to accomplish that. But usually, when I arrive late at night, I am exhausted. The implementation by FCCG was planned to take only four weeks, but we are now getting into our tenth week. I expect that I should feel a lot less busy soon.

Hank responds: "I will tell you something else too. Today I worked alongside customer service for a while and listened to a few phone calls. And I can tell you, it is total crap! Before they can get anything done, they have to ask permission from some kind of process coordinator person? I literally hear them tell customers on almost every call: 'I would like to arrange it for you, but I have to ask the coordinator what I can promise; I'll call you back soon!' Aren't they allowed to use their own brains anymore? That can't be true. Can they still go to the toilet without raising their hands and asking for permission? I guess not because that's inefficient!!"

What Hank just told me does sound very serious. It makes me realize that I hardly know what the effect of our new policy is on customers and the workplace. At 6:30 a.m., the first conference call with Pamela is scheduled. After that, I skip my usual morning walk of the office.

Wilma and Thom told me there were a few people complaining and resisting the changes, but this is to be expected. I expected a few carpenters complaining that "it is unworkable." Pamela also assured me that this kind of resistance is part of any change. Her advice was to continue to explain to people how the new process works and why it is better. After a while, they should see the benefits and will accept it. She said this is common with most of her customers. Shouldn't I be able to trust the recommendations of a reputable consultancy firm?

I tell Hank: "Of course, things have to speed up, Hank. That is also the reason that we are currently working on this acceleration program. I, too, want Formula Kitchen to be implemented as soon as possible. Or are you doubting my commitment? Why else do you think I spend so much time with FCCG to speed everything up? We are fully committed to Total Efficiency Management, and we are just reaping the first fruits!"

Hank is now visibly irritated: "Listen, Ronald, I don't care about your Total Ef-f*cking-cy Management. I know one thing for sure: maybe this works for a big supermarket chain, but not for a kitchen factory. And, ehh one more thing. You want to become a shareholder, yes? To be a shareholder you have to participate in the risk. Hiring expensive consultants that I must pay... where is your share in this?"

I am shocked by Hank's response. He continues: "I'll give you eight weeks to fix it. Otherwise, I will take over from you. We really have to deliver faster so we can keep our promise to the customer. Money is not an issue. I've told you that before. I have very deep pockets. Just tell me what the hell you need!"

Before I can say anything, he walks out of my room and leaves the building.

I am perplexed and slightly in panic. Damn! I thought we were doing so well. This could cost me my job and career. Who wants to hire a failed managing director? We have to change things quickly. We are indeed not a multinational.

I decide to cancel my remaining meetings today and drive home. I have to create some space to think.

Envelope

When I get home, I am surprised that Emily is not there, since it is her day off. Usually, she is studying all day. I go into the kitchen and prepare a strong espresso. I take it to my study. I take a seat and close my eyes to try to understand the situation. "Total Eff*ckingcy Management," Hank called it. I smile. He is right, somewhat.

When Pamela told her story about the roundabout and suggested using traffic controllers, I had unconsciously thought of an alternative. Namely: why don't we make the intersection simpler? Without traffic lights, people have to solve the problem themselves. Instead, all those coordinators ensure that our people no longer think for themselves. This makes decisions towards the customer even slower, while we have to go faster.

Emily scares the crap out of me when she suddenly throws an envelope on my desk. I didn't hear her come in. "This one was on the doormat," she says. "No sender address on it." Before I can ask her where she came from, she has already disappeared. I inspect the envelope. Indeed, only my name is on it: "For Ronald." That's all. No address and no stamp.

I open the envelope. Inside is a ticket for the Formula 1 race for the coming weekend, the Belgian Grand Prix. The ticket is personalized, as my name is printed on it. I take a good look at the access pass and see a shiny emblem with golden letters: "VIP Paddock Access." Wow, a VIP ticket! For Formula 1!!! That must have been pricey!

Other than the ticket, the envelope seems empty. Just to be sure, I hold it upside down and a small handwritten note falls out. I don't recognize the handwriting. The note reads: "Do you want to go faster? Take a look at Formula 1!"

Who sent this? Could this be from Pamela as a thank you for the project? Probably not, because then she would have handed it to me herself and she would probably have joined me. Maybe it was Hank? No, I don't think so either. After all, he is not so happy with me at the moment. Could it be a present from Emily? If that's true, why didn't she just say so? It makes no sense, given that I'm rarely at home these days. Then who was it? And why?

I stay still in my chair for a while. I just keep staring at the access pass. Completely surprised and amazed.

Who sent this to me...?

PART THREE

The Race

Charade

Sunday, early September

Sunday morning I leave home at 4:00 a.m. for the drive to the Spa Francorchamps circuit. Emily borrowed my car this weekend, so I drove her Prius there. During the drive, I realize she didn't actually tell me why she needs my car. I also forgot to ask her. Despite leaving on time, the trip is a lot longer than I expected.

I am just in time for the 4:30 a.m. shuttle train through the Channel Tunnel. All goes smoothly until the road becomes a lot busier around Liège. When I finally arrive in Verviers, the traffic becomes really heavy. I can feel that I've had a lot of stress lately. Everything hurts—my back, neck, and even my legs. My body clearly tells me that I can't keep up with this pressure for long.

The last part of the trip sends me over small winding roads, hills, and through forests. The navigation system tells me to turn left on the roundabout towards *Route-du-Circuit*. I arrive at the entrance of a large parking lot. A man, wearing an orange vest and carrying a walkie-talkie, redirects all the cars in front of me to another entrance. But when I show my VIP ticket, he says with a French accent: "Welcome, Monsieur Park! Come in, and park there à droite."

My parking area has tons of high-end cars. Sweet. I park the Prius between a Lamborghini and a shiny Porsche. I get out and can't help but take a picture of the situation and quickly send it to Emily. I start walking in the direction of a gate with a big sign — "VIPs Only" — above it.

At the gate I am welcomed by a friendly hostess with long blond hair, dressed in a dark blue overall from the Faster Racing team. Her overalls are full of logos from a variety of sponsors. In her hand, she holds a clipboard. She walks over to me and gives me a hand.

With a warm Flemish accent, she says: "Welcome, Mr. Park! I am your hostess for today and will now guide you inside." Apparently, the parking agent had already announced my arrival through his walkie-talkie.

I answer: "Please, call me Ronald!" She smiles kindly at me and scribbles something on her piece of paper. She hangs an access card around my neck.

"Would you please keep this card with you at all times? The circuit is divided into different safety zones. Without your pass, you may get into trouble. People would kill to get this pass. So please don't lose it." Her final remark is accompanied by a smile and a wink. She then precedes me. I'm impressed with the hospitality. I truly feel like a VIP!

We enter a dark tunnel that runs under the circuit. She turns to me and says: "We will soon be on the paddock, which is only accessible to drivers, team members, and special guests." We arrive at a security checkpoint where my bags are being searched.

When I'm on the other side I am amazed. It looks like a little city. Each team has erected its own building. Complete with roof terrace, bar, and restaurant. As we walk through the paddock, I keep looking around. There so much too much to see!

I recognize several people from TV: athletes, artists, actors, and famous entrepreneurs. The ones I don't recognize also look like they are famous. They parade with expensive clothing, shiny watches, and large sunglasses. It's all about seeing and being seen. Dozens of camera crews are interviewing people.

We arrive at the pavilion of the Faster Racing team. At the entrance, a waiter holds a tray full of champagne glasses. I gratefully accept one. Even though it is still morning, champagne fits perfect for this experience. The hostess says: "I will leave you here, Mr. Park. Lunch is almost ready. Afterward, I will pick you up for the VIP tour." With a smile, she turns around and disappears into the crowd.

I continue walking into the pavilion. In the back two chefs are busy cooking. The dishes they prepare look like they're from a Michelin star restaurant. Unbelievable. This must have cost a fortune. I'm looking around for a place to sit. At one of the tables, I see a familiar face. OMG, that's Tony Blair, the former prime minister! He is enthusiastically telling something and gesticulates with his arms. His four table companions, all in suits and ties, nod politely.

I feel out of place around all these celebrities. Me, a kitchen producer, at a VIP pavilion at Formula 1. It reminds me of what Emily says when I take her to a fancy restaurant: "Ronald, I think the food is great, but the charade of rich people makes me uncomfortable."

I take a seat at an empty table in the back of the room, where I have a good view of the whole pavilion. Almost automatically I pick up my phone and see if there is any news. Nothing special. The pavilion is now almost full, and two men in suits join me at my table. They are busy talking to each other in a language I don't understand... The three-course lunch is excellent, by the way.

A card with today's timetable stands on the table. The race is about to start. More and more people leave the pavilion in search of their grandstand seats. And when almost everyone is gone, the hostess arrives. She runs down a list of names and calls me: "Mr. Park! Ronald! Come on, it's time to go!"

Together with three other guests, I follow her outside. She guides us to the entrance of another building, protected by a security guard. He scans our VIP passes with a device and asks us to show a photo ID. I show my passport and enter through a narrow corridor.

A sliding door opens. Suddenly we are in the back of the pit box of Faster Racing. I see the two Formula 1 cars and dozens of technicians. The hostess says: "You will watch the race from here. Enjoy the experience!" Wow, I knew we would get a VIP tour, but I really didn't think I could get that close!

Amazement

There is so much to see in this pit box, I can't believe my eyes. At first, it seems a bit chaotic, so many people working in a tight space. But when I look more closely, I notice that everyone seems to know exactly what they have to do. There is no panic, no shouting or screaming. It all looks extremely professional and disciplined. Every move is graceful, yet quick. Deliberate, but with urgency. I reflect on how things are going in our office. This makes me sad. But that feeling quickly turns into optimism: there is a lot that can be improved. Wouldn't it be amazing if we could work this way too?

I see six engineers sitting at their computers, pointing at all kinds of numbers and graphs on their screens. One of them seems to take a break. He walks in our direction. Maybe he's coming over to us to chat? No, of course not, he has better things to do. But he is on his way to the coffee machine next to us. I take the plunge and ask him if I can also have a cup. This might not be allowed, but you miss 100 percent of the shots you don't take, right? He nods and presses the button for two double espressos on the coffee machine. The machine simultaneously fills two cups.

When he hands me the cup, I say: "Can I ask you something? What is on your computer screens?" The engineer's face lights up; he seems to appreciate my curiosity.

"I'm testing whether all sensors on the cars are working properly. We keep a close eye on the car during the race. For example, the brake temperature. If they get too hot, they stop working. We can then tell the driver over the onboard radio that he needs to use his engine more when slowing down, allowing the brake pads to cool down. In total, over a hundred sensors provide us with such information. Sometimes a sensor breaks down, so we test them before the start of the race so we don't have any surprises."

"Wow, unbelievable," I say. I am deeply impressed by the technology. "Over a hundred sensors that provide information?! But isn't that an impossible amount of work to monitor those? How many people are involved?"

The mechanic takes a sip of his coffee and smiles. I get the impression that I am not the first person to ask him such novice questions. He remains friendly and answers calmly: "There are sixty people working on the circuit. That is for both cars. We would love to bring in more people, but that is not allowed by the FIA. The rules state that sixty is the maximum. But not everyone has to be here physically. Dozens of colleagues are also participating live from the factory in England. We call that team our remote garage. These people see the same data in real-time and watch the camera feeds. They try to predict what the other teams will do. For example, they advise us when we should make a pit stop and install new tires."

I say: "So about a hundred people?"

The mechanic responds: "Yes, during the race there are about a hundred people working. But in total, our team consists of nearly a thousand colleagues who allow these two cars to be built and participate in the race."

My jaw drops in astonishment. "A thousand people! For two cars?

"The mechanic salutes me and says: "Yes, sir. At your service!" He turns around and walks back to his computer.

A while later, the two drivers enter the pit box. I notice how short they are. Just a little over 160 centimeters. And so young too. They seem deeply concentrated and are somewhat distant from the engineers. I see them throwing balls back and forth with someone who looks like their personal trainer. That seems like a smart exercise. It warms you up and it stimulates your reflexes at the same time. I can imagine reaction speed is just as important as warm muscles.

Later on, the two drivers put on their helmets and gloves. They get in their cars, which doesn't look like it is easy. They barely fit in there and are completely strapped. I suddenly understand why it is useful to be short as a driver.

The pit box has a peaceful vibe, but at the same time, you can feel the tension building up. It then becomes increasingly quiet. Suddenly, I hear a "VVVROOOOM!!!" The car engine fires up. What a deafening noise! I have never heard anything this loud! It's like a low-flying jet plane. That quiet was the calm before the storm.

I see one of the other guests make a small jump in the air out of distress. I was pretty shocked myself. Someone taps me on the shoulder and hands me earmuffs. I put them over my ears quickly.

The two cars follow each other out of the pit box, leaving behind a strange empty space. I'm able to understand everything that is going on. A large TV screen hangs in our corner of the pit box. And the earmuffs appear to be headphones because I can hear all kinds of voices. In the beginning, I have a hard time understanding them, because everything goes so fast. But after a while, I start to distinguish the voices and understand it much better. It's the team's radio. Everyone on the team is wearing headsets with a microphone. They are in constant communication with each other. I can hear everything they say to each other. I also occasionally hear the driver say something. This is amazing. I didn't expect that I could get this close. I feel enormously privileged.

On the TV screen, I see how the cars drive a lap around the circuit and park at the starting grid, where engineers prepare the cars for the start. Later, the engineers leave and the cars drive away for the warm-up lap. The drivers wobble their cars from left to right on the track. I remember seeing this on TV. This is how they warm up tires before the race starts. Warm tires provide more grip than cold ones.

The race will start soon. All the cars arrive at the starting grid. A voice on the on-board radio says: "The last car is on the grid. Start in five seconds." The starting lights turn red. I feel my heart rate go up and try to imagine how high the heart rates of the drivers must be.

The lights go out, and the cars go full throttle ahead. The twenty cars combined make an amazing noise. They quickly approach the first corner. It gives me goosebumps. It's going so fast. They brake at the very last moment. I feel the sweat in my hands. Whoops! One of the Faster Racing cars hit another car. A piece of the front wing breaks off. At first, I didn't notice. But in the slo-mo replay on the TV screen, we can clearly see it fly through the air.

The driver speaks on the radio: "I have damage on my front wing; please check the car." Followed by a short: "Copy that." Within twenty seconds, someone replies: "This is the remote garage. Wing end plate broken. Car still safe to drive. But the data predicts this will slow us down by half-a-second per lap. We recommend replacing the front wing as soon as possible." Then another confident voice responds: "Affirmative." Shortly thereafter, I hear a radio message directed to the driver: "Mark, box at the end of this lap. Box box. Please confirm." Within a second, the driver replies: "Coming in."

Only a minute and a half after the incident, about twenty mechanics run outside with their helmets on. They carry four new tires and a new front wing. After taking their positions, they wait for about fifteen seconds. The car comes to a halt, the tires are changed, and the damaged front wing is removed. A few seconds later, the installation of the new front wing is completed. The driver gets the green light, and the car shoots away. In total, he stood still for a mere ten seconds. The engineers give each other a high five; they are satisfied with their performance.

I follow the race with my jaw dropped, completely engaged. It is a spectacle. Half an hour later, there is another pit stop where only the tires are changed. This goes very quickly. The old tires are removed, and the new ones fitted in roughly two seconds!

I immediately think of what happens at my own tire care shop when I come in to fit my winter tires. I always have to wait at least half an hour at the reception. I thought this was pretty normal. But now that I've seen tires changed in two seconds, I wonder what they're doing in the remaining twenty-nine minutes and fifty-eight seconds. Imagine how it would be to get my tires changed in two seconds!

Faster Racing is a well-oiled machine with amazing teamwork. Dozens of people working simultaneously to achieve the same outcome. Everyone knows their duties and how it should be done. Everything is crystal clear. No need for discussion or lengthy meetings. And a team that is super proud of the work they do.

With my phone, I make a video of the replay of the pit stop on TV and send it to Wilma: "What would it be like if we could place a kitchen in this way? :-P"

Within a few seconds, she replies: "Sure, Ronald. You're starting to sound a bit like Hank. Dream on! ;-)"

Less than ninety minutes later, the race is over. Mark managed to finish in fourth place, despite his pit stop in the first round that dropped him back to the 20th position.

Post-Race Commentary

Mark climbs out of his racing car and takes off his gloves and helmet. Sweat runs down his face. A mechanic hands him a drinking bottle, which he empties in one go. Emily often says that motorsport is not a real sport. But if she saw this she would immediately agree that it requires some degree of athleticism.

One by one, Mark thanks his engineers and gives them a high-five. He walks further into the pit box and is now in close proximity to us. I manage to say something to him: "Hey, Mark, congratulations with the result. How did you manage to finish fourth in spite of the damage at the start? Why were you so fast?"

He looks at me and hesitates for a moment. Then a smile appears on his face: "It is actually common sense. Speed is a matter of simple physics."

This is not the answer I expected. "What do you mean?" I ask in surprise.

He says in a subtle tone: "Have you ever heard of Newton's second law? It said something very smart about acceleration."

I think for a moment. Newton's laws, that's a long time ago. I did not expect to receive a physics lesson from him. I stammer: "Uhh, I really can't remember. Can you please explain?"

Mark continues: "Newton's second law is $F = m \times a$. Or converted to acceleration: $a = F / m$. Acceleration is force divided by mass. We try to make our cars as light as possible. The less mass, the greater the acceleration. But beware: we cannot fall below the minimum weight. If the car is too light, we are disqualified by the FIA, who set the rules. Weight is calculated including the driver, that's why they put us on a scale before and after the race."

I nod. When watching TV, I always thought that was a bit strange. But it makes sense, I think. I now also understand why they bring their helmets to the scale, given that they wear them during the race.

Mark continues: "In order to accelerate, you can reduce mass to the minimum, but you can also increase the power of the engine. That is why it is so important for our team that we not only have a very reliable engine but also a very powerful one! Our engine currently delivers around 950 HP. That's quite a lot, but unfortunately, the other teams have an even stronger engine. You could conclude that we have no chance because of that. But that is not the case, because there is another force that works in opposition to the power of the engine: air resistance. If we manage to reduce it, then we will gain speed. Therefore, our team tries to lower the air resistance, and we have become quite good at that. But honestly, as a driver, I would prefer to have a little more horsepower from the engine!'

I understand. So it's not a matter of team tactics, cooperation, or a very good driver. No, ultimately simple physics determines the difference between winning and losing. I notice that Mark has to wrap up. There is an impatient lady behind him who wants to take him along. But I notice Mark seems to like explaining this to me.

He continues: "But that's not all. The lighter the car and the more powerful the engine, the greater the chance that you will miss a corner. Therefore we need downforce, which is produced by the wings on the car. The air resistance that is produced by the wings pushes me downwards so we can stick to the road. We need to balance the air resistance: low enough to go fast on the straights, but high enough to keep enough grip in the corners. To be quick, I try to brake as late as possible. In the beginning, it was pretty scary to drive towards a corner with 350 kilometers per hour and then brake very late. My father taught me how to do this when I was still driving go-karts. You have to slow down at the right moment to be able to go faster!"

Mark prepares to leave. Before he goes he says: "When the elementary physics are under control, then it is my turn. I ensure we're always driving in the right direction, responding quickly to changes, and making continuous steering adjustments. Anyway, I have to move on now, since our debriefing will start soon. Enjoy the rest of the day!"

I thank him and need a few seconds to process what Mark just said. It is all a bit much. I cannot decide whether what he explained was just very obvious or super brilliant. Probably the latter. I realize that Mark is a special kid!

From where I am standing I can peek into the room where Mark has walked in. It's some kind of conference room with a long table, where about thirty people sit with laptops and headphones. I realize that the remote garage also participates in that meeting remotely. Mark sits down on the empty chair at the head of the table. Cool, I can also listen to what is being said via my headset! In the minutes that follow, I hear them go through a checklist. "How did the brakes feel? How was the gearbox? What did you notice on the balance?" Mark is being questioned. Every element is discussed in detail with the entire team. However, I don't understand most of what they are talking about. Many terms are jargon to me. Yet I find it very interesting to listen. Especially the extent to which they scrutinize everything that happened.

I was deeply listening, I completely lost track of time. Suddenly I realize that they have been talking for more than an hour and a half, and they don't even seem ready yet. I decide to walk back to the pavilion. Once in the restaurant, I take a look at the menu. Tomorrow's workday is going to be stressful, so I decide to enjoy myself.

Team Captain

After dessert, I see the team boss of the Faster Racing team walking through the pavilion. He has straight brown hair and a thinly trimmed beard. His name is Edwin, and I think he is in his mid-forties. I heard somewhere that he married a pop star, but I don't remember exactly which one. He passes almost all tables and greets many people. The race is over, but apparently, his day is not nearly finished yet. He shakes hands and takes photos with numerous guests. Our former prime minister also takes a selfie with him. A few moments later, the pavilion starts to become empty. I'm also ready to go, but when I see Edwin sitting on the corner of the bar, I can't contain my curiosity and go to him. I approach him hesitantly: "Say, Ed, can I ask you something?"

He yawns a bit, stretches himself, and then responds quite energetically: "Sure. What can I do for you?"

I continue: "My name is Ronald Park, and I was in the pit box with you during the race."

Edwin looks at me questioningly: "Ah yes, now I recognize you. I saw you even talked to Mark for a while, between the race and the debriefing. He rarely does that; Mark usually immediately shoots into the meeting room."

I enjoy hearing it was special. It felt special to me, and even Edwin had noticed. I ask: "I listened to your debriefing through my headset. And I noticed that the conversation lasts almost longer than the entire race. Why do you spend so much time on this?"

Edwin looks at me in surprise as if I just asked a stupid question. "Well, it actually is common sense. Do I really have to explain it?"

I remember Mark said something similar. "Uhh, yes please, if you could," I answer.

Edwin first waves at a bartender for a drink, who seems to immediately know what he wants. Then he says: "If you improve a little every day, time will solve all your problems. Moreover, all racing teams do it, so if you do not improve continuously, you will be chasing them in no time." I look at him with a questioning expression.

"During the debriefing, we discuss what can be improved next time. We earn back the time we invest in this. And that's not all we do. During the race weekend, we have a fixed rhythm with over fifty moments we use to reflect and learn."

Fifty of these meetings per weekend? That can't be true. That's even worse than all the meetings I have with FCCG every week.

The bartender hands Edwin a can of soda. He takes a sip and continues: "Tonight we will be transporting the entire circus to the circuit in Italy, where we will race the coming weekend. This leaves us about four days to build an improved car. Using the collected data and the things that we learned during the debrief, I expect we will make about 750 small and large improvements before the next race."

I'm amazed. "That many? 750?!? How do you accomplish that so quickly?"

"The trick is to make our cycle time as short as possible. That is the time that it takes to get from an idea to a working, tested, and improved car part. The faster that goes, the more innovations we can put on the car before the next race. Then we can experience which updates really make the car faster in practice. That is why the free practice sessions on Friday are so incredibly important for us. There we learn what works and what doesn't."

He now starts sounding like some kind of management guru. I wonder if I should start making notes, but I don't have a pen or paper.

Edwin takes another sip and continues: "It is essential that everyone in the factory knows what the priorities are. That is why we have an all-hands meeting every Monday morning where we discuss what we have learned. Everyone is present. And because then everyone knows what the priorities are, the work actually happens automatically."

I say, in disbelief: "Sure. With a thousand people? Only a few hundred people work in my company, but nothing happens automatically in our place."

He quaffs the rest of his drink and pauses before softly saying: "Yes, we were in a similar situation a while back. A few years ago it didn't go well at all. We were unable to finish in the top 10. Our shareholders became impatient and put the thumbscrews on. I kept a tight grip and put a lot of pressure on my people. I was on top of everything myself and made sure that nobody was slacking. When things didn't improve, I hired a race consultant who I made responsible for analyzing and improving the processes. That actually made the situation worse because he introduced all kinds of complicated procedures."

This sounds awfully familiar. Then he even starts to whisper: "I will tell you something that not many people know. The pressure on my shoulders became too much for me. I became overwhelmed and I could no longer think clearly. I saw my wife and children less and less often, so the home front also stopped supporting me. Eventually, I ended up in the hospital with serious pneumonia."

I gulped out of shock—it sounds like he's talking about me. The last thing I want is needing to be admitted into a hospital. I feel I have to be careful. I ask: "Wow! What did you do?"

Edwin: "Well, it was when I was in the hospital I realized that acceleration is a matter of simple physics."

I say, concisely, "Let me guess: acceleration is power divided by mass?"

His eyes light up, and he reacts enthusiastically: "Yes exactly! How did you know? Oh, I get it: Mark, right?!? Ha, yes I talked to him about that yesterday. Newton's laws are the basis for car racing. But just like a car, a racing team itself must be light and agile. There is simply no time for bureaucracy. The less mass in your organization, the easier you can accelerate. I keep the organization lean and simple. One of the ways we achieve this is by asking this question during our weekly meeting: 'What is in the way of being able to do your work?' We then discover all sorts of things that we can scrap or simplify: unnecessary procedures or approval processes, handover moments, other meetings, etcetera. Those things were once installed for good reason, but often no longer needed. Often we can reach its purpose in a much simpler way. And if you can completely remove it, that is even better. Less really is more!"

I suddenly think of what Mark, the driver, said: elementary physics. Mass slows you down! Remove things to become faster. Brilliant! When things are not going well, I often intervene by adding rules or implement changes. Omitting things is, of course, also a possibility, maybe a better one.

We chat for a long time. Time seems to stand still; I forget everything around me. In addition to mass, we also talk about force.

Edwin says enthusiastically: "Over the years, I have learned that as a manager you can't tug an entire organization alone. Your natural urge is to want to know everything, make decisions about everything, and tell people exactly what to do. Even if you are the smartest or strongest man on earth, that's not possible. In an organization, everyone has to put their shoulders to the wheel and use their thinking power. That only becomes possible if I dare to trust my people. So use their collective intelligence. I do that by ensuring that everyone is involved, takes responsibility, and acts accordingly."

This sounds like a fairy tale to me. I respond: "Employees who take responsibility and are involved. They are involved, but they are mainly concerned with themselves and their own department. They do whatever they want and don't seem to care about what we are trying to achieve with the company. I've been trying to change this for years, but somehow I just can't succeed. They don't seem to want it."

He looks at me again as if I'm stupid: "Well, actually, it's very simple, Ronald. If you keep micromanaging, people will lean back. If you want involved employees, you just have to involve them!"

I smile, thinking this could be a tile quote. If you want involved people then you just have to involve them.

Edwin looks at his watch and suddenly grabs his bag in a hurry. He says: "I have to get going; I'm already late. Good luck with it, Ronald! And remember: you can't make people take responsibility; they need to want to take it themselves." He gets up and walks straight out of the pavilion. I call out to him: "Yes, but then how?" but he doesn't respond.

I look at the empty can of soda and see that he has left his business card with his mobile number. I quickly put it in my pocket.

Quit While You're Behind

My mind is restless. I learned so much and am super inspired! I never anticipated this when I drove here this morning. Whether I can do something with it in practice remains to be seen, but I think it would be a good idea to capture some notes.

I ask the bartender for a double espresso and ask if he has a pen and paper for me. The pen is not a problem, but he doesn't have any paper. He hands me a napkin instead. It does not matter to me. They are firm enough to write on it.

As I drink my coffee slowly, I think about everything Edwin and Mark said to me today and I try to summarize it for myself:

- Accelerate by reducing mass or increasing power.
- Lightweight organization: remove things or simplify.
- Provide trust and let people take responsibility.
- Slow down to change direction.
- Move in the right direction, respond quickly, and steer continuously.
- Improve every day so eventually, time will solve everything.
- A meeting rhythm to reflect and learn.
- Shorten cycle time from idea to product.
- Everyone must know the purpose and what the priorities are.
- Use collective power and intelligence.
- Get involved people by involving them.

I look at the list. I'm pretty satisfied. It will take a while before I understand what this means for our company. I'm trying to figure out what we can do with this. What's the first step? When I look at the top three points, the penny suddenly drops.

Those process coordinators are actually just additional mass. Process coordinators do not assemble kitchens. Why would things become faster through more coordination? It doesn't make sense to me now. After the conversation with Hank, I already had my doubts about the approach, but this insight is the drop that overflows the bucket.

I pick up my phone and call Pamela. Even though it is Sunday evening, she answers her phone immediately. She didn't mind, she said; she was working anyway.

I tell her that we will immediately stop implementing Total Efficiency Management and that I'm ending the collaboration with FCCG. We are going to do it on our own from now on. She reacts fiercely but does not seem completely surprised. She raises her voice on the phone, but her reaction doesn't seem very genuine. She tries to persuade me to continue for a few weeks since it would be foolish to stop now. In her mind, we're almost there; stopping now would be giving up right before the finish line. I reconfirm that I've made my decision.

In the meantime, I had calculated the amount of additional temporary workers I could hire with the saved money. I can hire at least four new colleagues for every consultant. And consultants don't assemble kitchens!

The conversation with Pamela ends abruptly. She suddenly says: "I have to hang up, Ronald. I have to make an international conference call. I will immediately pull back our people. But the invoice is on its way. I wish you all the best." I hear a click and a tone indicating that the call has been terminated. This is no way to treat a customer, is it? We would never just hang up, would we? I make a short note to check this with Laura.

I decide to write an email to the entire company:

```
From: Ronald
To: Everyone
Subject: Crisis meeting: all hands on deck

Hello all,

I hope you had a good weekend.

I expect you all Monday morning at 9:00 a.m.
in the canteen for an important meeting. We
are changing course. The implementation of
Total Efficiency Management will be reversed
immediately. I look forward to explaining the
new approach.

It would be great if all of you are able to
be there!

See you tomorrow,

Ronald
```

It is getting pretty dark outside when I walk out of the pavilion. Apparently, the conversation with Edwin took longer than I thought. It feels special that he was willing to spend so much time with me.

Somehow I feel a strange kind of relief. I'm excited. I am looking forward to a new start.

The parking lot is already largely empty. But the Prius is patiently waiting for me. I chuckle at the thought of all those other VIP guests with all their fancy cars. I get in the car and turn on the music. I drive towards the exit of the parking lot. The friendly parking guard of this morning is nowhere to be seen.

The drive back home is a lot smoother than the journey there. During the trip, I am overwhelmed by a feeling of gratitude. Especially because of the personal story that Edwin shared with me. And I am grateful to Emily for everything she has tolerated from me lately and how she has supported me unconditionally. It is quite special and something that I don't think about often enough. Along the way, I stop to buy flowers for her.

Just after midnight, I arrive home. I place the flowers in a vase on the kitchen table.

I walk up the stairs to the bathroom to brush my teeth. On the shelf above the sink is an empty strip of Emily's birth control pills. I throw it in the trash without thinking. Emily is already sleeping. I slide between the sheets as gently as possible. She doesn't seem to notice. I lie awake for a while and think back on the long and very impressive day.

Despite the tiredness, I am very happy that I went. It was an experience to never forget!

PART FOUR

Restart

Weekstart

I spend the night tossing and turning. The thoughts keep spinning in my head. I can't stop thinking about yesterday, the conversation with team boss Edwin, and what I will say later during the meeting with my colleagues. I watch the time ticking away on my alarm clock. As soon as it shows 5:00 a.m., I decide to get up and go to the office. I quietly put my clothes on in the dark, so that Emily does not wake up.

When I arrive at the office, I jump out of the car. It is cold and very dark, and the parking area is completely empty. Using my keys, I raise the roller door and turn on the main power switch. It takes a few minutes before the fluorescent light tubes are at their full strength.

I go to my room and open my laptop to check my email. Six hundred and eighty-seven unread messages. Ugh. Strangely enough, I only see one reply to the email I sent yesterday. It's from Laura from customer service: "Thank you for finally seeing this, Ronald. Those consultants were only concerned with our internal stuff and not with the customer. I hope we will focus all our attention on the customer from now on!"

I start preparing a PowerPoint for the meeting later on. I'm excited. Time flies when I'm working on it. When I pour my fourth espresso of the day, I look at my watch. Whoops, it's already a quarter to nine! I hurry to the canteen.

When I arrive there, I am surprised that it is almost completely empty. Only Wilma is there, busy typing on her laptop in the corner at a table. She looks at me and says, somewhat skeptically: "Have you had fun in Belgium?"

ꙮ

At five past nine, the canteen is only half full. More than half of the employees did not show up. I had hoped for a larger turnout, even though I only sent the email very late last night. I decide to wait another minute before I start. My managers are all here, thankfully.

I start: "Thank you all for coming." A few employees look around demonstratively, looking for the rest of their colleagues, but when they don't see them, they shrug their shoulders.

I show the first slide of my presentation on the screen. "Look, we all know by now that Total Efficiency Management is not working well for us. With the arrival of the process coordinators, there has been some improvement in the lead time, but it is not enough." The slide shows a graph: from twelve to sixteen to ten weeks. I say urgently: "The goal is to really get the delivery time to fourteen days. We are now at ten weeks. That is seventy days and far too long. Do you realize the challenge we are facing?" The group stares at me in silence.

Convinced of my plan, I decide to go further: "This weekend I thought deeply about how things can be done differently, and as you have read in my email, I have decided to stop the FCCG process coordinators. Instead, I would like to use your thinking power: from now on we will all put our shoulders to the wheel. I know that other organizations benefit greatly from a weekstart ceremony in which all people in the company are required to meet. And that is why I would like to introduce that to us. From now on we will meet every Monday morning. Is this clear, or does anyone have a question?"

Nobody says anything. Are they ~~be~~ afraid to open their mouths? The uncomfortable silence makes me anxious. After a silence that seemed as long as an eternity (in reality, it was probably five seconds), one of the customer service employees slowly raises his hand. He says: "Ronald, I can't help asking you: where did you get this? Have you read a new management book or something?" A number of employees chuckle softly.

I respond: "Well, if you really want to know, I went to Formula 1 this weekend and saw how things can be done differently."

He looks at me with a scowl and says: "Pfff as if we are a racing team. Our company is completely different. We build kitchens. And pretty slowly too. What exactly does a weekstart solve? It only consumes time. Time we do not spend on our work. That long delivery time, that's really the management's problem. I think we as employees should just do our jobs, and you, the management, should do your jobs. You have decided that it must go faster? Then just tell how! I really don't understand what it will solve if we all meet together."

I feel embarrassed. I have to try my best to suppress my irritation. "Well, look, I want you to be committed and take responsibility for the situation. It's really not just the management's problem..."

Before I can finish, the customer service colleague shouts angrily: "Do you really mean that? I am working my ass off, and you say that I am not committed?! I recently started working evenings because someone decided a kitchen had to be placed for the crown princess! I helped to install kitchens at other clients', while that is not even my job! And when you had your celebration, we were not even invited. You were there with your entire management team, partying and drinking at our expense. I can't take this bullshit anymore!" After he has finished, he angrily walks out of the canteen. Laura goes after him.

Shit. How am I supposed to solve this? It feels like the whole group is ready to go after me. What did Edwin, the team boss, say again? "You can't force people to take responsibility." I realize that my proposal is a bit like forcing them. I think for a moment and continue in a serious tone: "Listen. I understand that the past few weeks have been very tough. And I really see that everyone works really hard. I really appreciate that. I see the point he made about the party. We should indeed have celebrated the accomplishment with everyone, not only with the people who were on the special project. We will do that differently next time. I promise."

I wait a while to see if there are any reactions, but nothing happens. The group seems to calm down a bit. It seems that my different tone helped to connect with them. I continue: "But it's not about working harder. That is not the solution. More effort will never shorten the delivery time from ten weeks to two weeks. We have to work smarter instead of harder. I am convinced that this is only possible if we all think together. We must use our collective intelligence!! Linking all our brains together. Not just mine and the management team—everyone. So also yours, and yours, and yours!" As I say this, I point my finger at a few employees.

I continue: "At every weekstart, I want us to reflect on the question: what is in your way to be able to go even faster? If we do that every time, week after week, we will get better and faster, step by step. So, I would like to ask you now, who has a concrete idea?"

"I know something!" It sounds from the back of the canteen. It is someone who works in the Placement department. "Well, I want the guys at production to work a bit more accurately. Because very often when I am placing a kitchen at a customer's house, the cupboards just don't fit well. I try to solve it on the spot by trimming something or filling up an empty space, but often that doesn't work. Sometimes I even have to disassemble half of the kitchen and send back certain parts to production, so they can solve their error. It takes at least a week before the parts come back and I can finish the job."

Now that a concrete improvement idea is being suggested, I feel relieved and energized. But that is short-lived.

From the other side of the canteen, one of the carpenters of Production responds aggressively: "Wait a minute! We receive the measurements from the planning department, and then we simply produce it by that specification. We are very accurate and precise to the millimeter. If the kitchen does not fit, then you should not blame us, but them!"

In front of the room, I see the face of a colleague from Planning turn red. She turns to the carpenter and says firmly: "We work with standard sizes that we have agreed on with you! It is not our fault. We receive the order from Sales, and it says exactly what the customer has ordered. So I suspect something goes wrong in the Sales process."

One of the sales managers, clearly recognizable as such by his neat suit and tightly gelled hair, says: "Yeah, sure, blame Sales again. It is always our fault. Bring it on. But thanks to whom do you all have a job? Who makes sure the company can even exist? Exactly. That's us!! So keep on whining and blaming us."

I look in the direction of Paul and see that he looks down at the floor and shakes his head. Apparently, we are worse off than I thought. Of course, shouting back and forth between departments in the canteen doesn't make it better. And it immensely annoys me that nobody takes responsibility for this quality problem.

I interrupt the discussion and say something that I know I'll regret later: "That's enough! These types of errors are really unacceptable from now on. Today I want us to get to the bottom of this and find the cause. By the end of the week, this should be fixed; otherwise, heads will roll! I want to know exactly who is responsible for these mistakes."

The canteen is quiet. Terribly quiet. I decide to close the meeting quickly: "Okay, everyone. Back to work! And see you next week!"

Pfffff... I wonder if Faster Racing's weekstart is similar. It all sounded so beautiful, but I didn't expect that I would encounter so much resistance. This weekend I saw what it can be like when everything is tightly organized, but how do we get there? One thing is certain: it cannot go on like this anymore, because then I might go under myself, just like Edwin. And I certainly won't let that happen!

As soon as I get home in the evening, I immediately receive a big hug from Emily: "How sweet of you that you have brought flowers, Ronald." During dinner, we finally have time to catch up. Emily is very curious about what I experienced at the Formula 1 Grand Prix. She seems even more interested when I elaborate on the idea of collective intelligence, and she immediately starts spouting ideas about it. Coincidentally, this has exactly been the subject of Emily's previous day of training.

I notice I don't pay attention to what Emily is saying because my head is still full of the disastrous weekstart that morning. I tell Emily that it didn't go according to plan at all. She responds with a smile: "Ha, that reminds me of what Mike Tyson, the boxer, once said: *'eveyone has a plan until they get punched in the face!'*" A punch in the face, yes, that's exactly how it felt.

Emily asks me if she can give me some feedback about the situation. "Yes, of course," I respond, somewhat surprised that she first asks me. I have noticed that as a director I don't get honest, direct feedback from my colleagues that often, so it's always nice when Emily holds a mirror in front of me.

She tells me that she suspects I stepped into my old pitfall: under pressure, I become rather directive and bossy. Ouch, it hurts to hear that. I set the intention to let go more and give my managers more space. It is a nice and pleasant evening. Emily decides to leave her study books closed. And I don't grab my laptop for a change. Emily doesn't talk about children either, this time. And that's nice. Because often that ends up with both of us going to bed angry. I do forget to ask her why she wanted to use my car. And Emily didn't talk about that either.

Finger-Pointing

T ime for our weekly management meeting. As a director, I notice that I often speak a lot, and therefore there is not always room for others' ideas. I want to change that, so I asked Emily yesterday for advice on how I could do that. She came up with something she had learned during her training: opening the meeting with a so-called "check-in round."

It works as follows: at the start of the meeting, everyone, one by one, answers the question: "What has your attention?" It is not intended that you set off a long monologue or report on all your current projects. Instead, the idea is that everyone shares what he or she currently has on their mind, with the aim of getting present and focusing their attention on the meeting ahead. It may be work-related, but it is also a good idea to share something more personal, such as: "I have a terrible headache so I apologize if I'm more irritable than usual," or "I received the key to our new house yesterday, so I am very happy but also somewhat distracted by how I should handle the move."

If someone shares, the others listen. We do not delve deeply into what is being shared. Emily said that because everyone makes their voices heard, you get closer to each other as human beings, and that enhances the quality of the collaboration and the group fosters a "shared consciousness." She compared it to "tuning an orchestra before the concert."

I kick off the check-in round: "What has my attention is that I am very excited to tell you what I saw at Formula 1 this weekend and to get started with you. In addition, I am very disappointed with how the weekstart went yesterday."

We continue the round and get a glimpse into where everyone's head is. I hear things I hadn't realized.

For example, Wilma and Thom are mainly busy digesting my choice to stop process coordination, and what that means for their department. The joint off-site and the implementation of Total Efficiency Management felt good: a sense of control and clarity through a proven method. But now that that has been abandoned, this brings uncertainty.

During the check-in, Paul shares that he should be incredibly happy and cheerful because there have been so many additional sales in the showrooms. But that he also is puzzled over how he can get his salesmen to stop selling kitchens like idiots, as he now realizes that more orders mean more trouble. Laura indicates that she is worried about the low morale in her department. It was already bad due to the number of complaints from customers, but the disastrous weekstart has only made it worse.

I give the team a short update of my inspiration from the weekend before. I tell them what I noticed at the Formula 1 circus. The napkin with notes comes in handy. I explain what team boss Edwin told me about the weekstart and how important it is for them to align everyone around the most important things. My managers are quite positive about the idea of a weekstart, even though the first one went dramatically yesterday. We simply decide to try it a few times to see how it unfolds.

The atmosphere is good; there is a lot of understanding between each other. Until I ask Wilma, who is responsible for placement, to say more about the situation with the cupboards that don't always fit.

She looks up frightened from her laptop and says: "Yes, I have sorted things out. There are a lot of handovers between us and production, but that isn't the problem. And it also isn't the planning who is to blame. It's actually very clear to me what the cause is: sales has recently stopped making blueprints."

I am surprised and look at Paul. He reacts, clearly irritated: "Yes, that's right, our salesmen and saleswomen used to visit the customer to measure up, but that cost us too much capacity. We saw that potential customers left the showrooms because they had to wait too long for an available salesman. We then adjusted our process and since then asked the customer to take a photo of the room where the kitchen will be placed and to measure it themselves. In the showroom, we then create a rough drawing of the situation. Then we quickly close the deal. This really goes much faster. And speed is what we need!"

Wilma, Thom, and Laura let out a loud sigh. But I respond cheerfully: "It's great that we found the leak. And let's see it positively. Now that we know what the problem is, we can solve it. Can't you go back to the original process, Paul? This also immediately solves your other problem: you said during the check-in that your salesmen are selling too much, right? So the solution seems obvious!"

Before Paul can respond, Thom interrupts me: "The measurements must be technically sound. I don't believe salesmen can make accurate blueprints."

Paul says: "Yes, you're right, Thom; my salesmen are not trained for that. They just want to close deals. And ultimately that's exactly what I am accountable for!"

Laura rolls her eyes and says, "It would be much better if you just closed a few fewer deals. We can't handle all those new orders, can we?"

It doesn't feel like we're getting closer to a solution. I ask Wilma: "Could your team make the blueprints? Then you'll be faced with fewer surprises when installing the kitchen. You'll be more in control that way."

Wilma responds to my question, surprised: "We also need to do that? No, we're completely overloaded with work. Driving to the customer one more time to measure up the kitchen will at least take half a day, and we don't have that capacity at the moment."

I look at Thom: "And what if your team would do it? After all, you have the technical knowledge to do it well."

He responds quickly as if he had already prepared his answer: "No. After all, Sales closes the deal so they have to agree on the right size with the customer. And I don't want to be blamed when things go wrong."

Laura interrupts: "In addition, we are not solving our current biggest problem that way. The problem is that we are selling too much! And as a result, the customers shit all over us!"

We are not getting any further. Everyone blames each other. I believe the biggest problem with our company is not that we sell too much. That can't be the problem, can it? A company that claims to have a problem because customers want to buy too much? These are luxury problems. If we would sell too little, that would be a problem!

I say cynically: "Okay, sure, then I will call Hank that we know what the problem is: our company is in trouble because we sell too much. You've got to be kidding me. That makes no sense!" I try again: "What could be a solution?"

It stays quiet. It looks like they expect me to take charge and make a decision. That's what I always do if we can't figure it out. But I want them to take responsibility themselves. How can I let them do that? Should we vote and then let the majority decide? That wouldn't work either. After all, they all want something different. I break the silence and say: "We can still spend hours discussing this, but we don't have that time."

Paul gets up, looks at his expensive watch, and says in a smart tone: "In fact, the hour is already well over. And I have to go to a new customer who wants to order a large custom-built kitchen. Good luck all of you and see you next week!" The others also stand up and walk away. I end up sitting in an empty meeting room, between several half-empty cups of coffee.

Frustrated, I walk to my office and close the door behind me. I think deeply and try to imagine what team boss Edwin would do in this situation. Then it occurs to me: why don't I just ask him? I find his business card and dial his number. But unfortunately, I get his voicemail.

I record a message: "Listen, Edwin, thanks for our conversation this weekend. I learned a lot. I'm now trying to involve my people, but they don't seem to want to take responsibility for the situation. Learning from mistakes is also not going well. Do you have any tips or ideas as to how I can make them understand?"

I take a moment to reflect and read through my notes from the Formula 1 weekend again. My next step suddenly becomes clear to me. I open my laptop and start typing:

```
From: Ronald
To: Everyone
Subject: MANDATORY: Friday evaluation and
Monday ALL hands on deck

Hello all,

Yesterday morning not everyone was at the
weekstart. I can understand because it was
announced last minute, but on Monday at 9:00
a.m. I expect everyone.

To get through this crisis, we must all be
involved in improving our process. That's why
I urge you all to meet with your department
next Friday to reflect on these questions:

•   What is in your way to speed up?
•   If you had a magic wand and you could
    change one thing about how we work, what
    would it be?
•   What would you do if this were your own
    company?

During the weekstart on Monday, we'll go
through the answers. I count on your presence!

See you Monday,

Ronald
```

Decision Tree

Sunday afternoon

oday I watch the Italian Formula 1 Grand Prix. When you watch the race on TV, you don't see much about what happens behind the scenes. I remember Edwin said they were making 750 improvements per race! Our progress has been very limited in the meantime.

"Ronald!" Emily shouts. "There is a deliveryman at the door and he wants you to place your signature." Huh, what can that be? I walk to the door, grab the little plastic pen, and scribble on the small window on his device. The courier hands me a large yellow cardboard envelope. I pull the strip to tear it open. The first thing that comes out of it is a postcard. It is a photo of the circuit in Francorchamps. There is a single sentence on the back. "You learn by doing rather than thinking about doing!" The card is not signed. There is something else in the envelope: a page that looks like it was torn from a book. It is a kind of step-by-step plan. In fact, it looks like a decision tree.

There is no sender on the outside either. Very strange. Who sent me this? And why? Could it be Edwin, following my voicemail? Cool!! I read the page carefully.

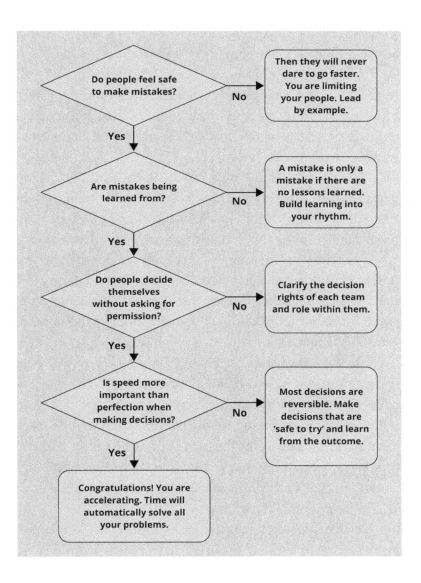

Do people feel safe to make mistakes?

No → Then they will never dare to go faster. You are limiting your people. Lead by example.

Yes ↓

Are mistakes being learned from?

No → A mistake is only a mistake if there are no lessons learned. Build learning into your rhythm.

Yes ↓

Do people decide themselves without asking for permission?

No → Clarify the decision rights of each team and role within them.

Yes ↓

Is speed more important than perfection when making decisions?

No → Most decisions are reversible. Make decisions that are 'safe to try' and learn from the outcome.

Yes ↓

Congratulations! You are accelerating. Time will automatically solve all your problems.

What I read initially conflicts with what I believe. If people don't dare to make mistakes, then I am "limiting" my people? Pff… What nonsense! That would be nice and easy. If someone makes a mistake, then it's my fault. So I'm causing all the problems in the company? Yeah, right.

"A mistake is only a mistake if there are no lessons learned," it says. That sounds like a platitude. "Build learning into your rhythm." We have already started this: departments evaluate on Friday what could be improved, and on Monday we share it with each other.

"Do people decide for themselves without asking permission?" No, I don't think so. The paper then advises to clarify decision rights, probably so they no longer need permission? That sounds pretty logical. I wonder if all our employees know what they already can decide for themselves. In fact, I think my own management team doesn't even know that. That is why they ask me for permission all the time. Often for the simplest things. I've never thought about it that way. This is interesting.

"Most decisions are reversible," it says. Now that's an insight! You can indeed make a decision and then reverse it later. Then we don't have to worry too much about it. And if you don't mind making mistakes along the way, you learn a lot. Make it "safe to try," it says. Promising on TV that you can deliver something that you have never achieved does not sound "safe to try," but in hindsight, we maybe could have done a first pilot or something.

"Decide quickly and steer continuously"; I remember Mark saying something similar. I recognize something else that Edwin said: "If you accelerate, time will automatically solve all your problems." Could this be a page from Faster Racing's internal company handbook? I turn around the page to look at the back, but there is nothing there. I have no idea where this came from. But it is definitely food for thought. I can incorporate these insights nicely in the weekstart tomorrow.

I show the page to Emily. "How interesting!" she says. "This could come from one of my course books. It looks like a mix of Sociocracy and Holacracy."

It sounds like she suddenly has started speaking Russian. I frown at her and jokingly say: "You sound a bit holy crazy yourself now!'

She immediately reacts very fiercely and emotionally: "Are you making fun of me? Oh, well, I don't care. Is it so hard to believe I could help you with something for once? You only think about yourself. Enjoy watching TV!" She storms off.

I am left a bit dazed by her sudden eruption. Where did this come from? I was just kidding...

Only then do I notice the sound of the television. Damn! I forgot the whole race. I quickly sit down and watch the TV. The drivers are on the podium celebrating with champagne. It looks like Mark ended in third place.

Resources

Monday morning, 9:00 a.m.

ime for the weekstart. This time I don't have any slides. I push a large wheeled whiteboard into the canteen. The room is full this time; that's nice. "Good morning, everyone. Did you have a good weekend?" Silence. "Not really? Well, I did!" I say cheerfully.

"All right, let's get started. Last time we discussed that I would like to involve you so that we can look for solutions together. I thought about it again this weekend and I'd like to share three principles that I think can help us."

I start writing on the whiteboard and go through them one by one:

1. *If we try to become faster, then we will make more mistakes.*
2. *Learning from mistakes is more important than finding the culprit.*
3. *Speed is more important than perfection.*

I see a doubtful look on my colleagues' faces. I decide to continue with my story: "And I would like to set a good example by telling you the biggest mistake I made last week."

For a moment, I hesitate to continue. Will they think I am weak? Eventually, I force myself to carry on: "During the previous weekstart, I reacted rather angrily when I heard that placement often received cupboards that didn't fit. I then said that heads would roll. I really shouldn't have said that, and I'd like to apologize for that. Now I am only human and I also make mistakes, but still. In this company, no one will be fired for making a mistake. Never! You need to make mistakes to be able to learn. The faster we make them, the faster we learn. That is crucial! I've committed myself to take a more inquisitive attitude next time. Can you please help me remind me of this when I say something stupid again?"

Everyone looks at me completely surprised, but nobody says anything. I continue. "Did you meet with your team on Friday to reflect on how things went last week? And what you believe is in the way to speed up?" A few heads nod. "Good, who wants to share something?"

Paul "Mr. Teflon" is the first to raise his hand. I ask: "Okay, Paul, what would you do if this were your company? What would you change?"

He responds: "Well, I decided with the sales team on Friday that from now on we will scan the order forms immediately after the customer has signed because we used to lose them sometimes. After a week or two, some customers called to ask about the status of their order. And this counted towards the delivery time; what a waste! So from now on, we scan and email them immediately so we don't forget them anymore. An order is only an order once it has been mailed to planning!"

I respond, "Very good, Paul. Is there anyone else who wants to share something?"

A number of other improvements are shared. Sometimes by one of my management team members, but often by colleagues from the departments themselves. For example, a customer service colleague says that they have ordered a few new headsets because the connection sometimes dropped out with the old ones—very annoying for both the customer and the agents.

I notice that nobody from production, Thom's department, speaks up. I ask Thom directly: "And what about production?" He shakes his head to indicate that they have nothing. But someone behind him raises his hand and starts talking. It's a man in a blue overalls with a pencil behind his ear. He says in frustration: "All the rules in our department make me crazy. Forms. Processes. The memos from the planning department are the worst. I have often told the boss that we should stop doing that so that our work can be done much faster, but nothing happens."

Thom "The Saw" turns around. He appears blindsided as if this is new information to him. Paul, who is also responsible for the planning department next to sales, is also surprised. I realize that this is exactly what I want to happen: that people can express their concerns and improvement ideas without being dismissed by managers.

"Thank you for sharing!" I shout enthusiastically. "I would love to hear more about this later and would like to see whether we can find a solution for it together. Will you be able to stick around for a moment?" The carpenter nods.

I decide it's enough for today and ask: "Anyone else?" It remains silent. "Okay then, see you all next week."

The room is emptied. The carpenter, Thom, and Paul are left behind. I shake hands with the carpenter: "Hi, can you remind me of your name again?"

The handshake is very firm; he almost demolishes my hand. "Hello, boss. I am Nelson."

Thom and Paul are a bit uncomfortable and seem to be bracing themselves for what will come next. Apparently, they are afraid that I will reprimand them, but that is not at all what I intend to do. I ask: "Okay, Nelson, tell me, what do you think should change?"

Nelson takes a deep breath and talks as if Thom and Paul are not there: "We are being treated like children. Not as craftsmen. I'll give an example. If I need new gloves, I must first go to my boss for permission. I first have to juggle for a time in his schedule to meet with him. He is always in meetings, and we can't simply walk in to ask a question. One or sometimes two days later, he has time to meet. He then gives me a memo, which I have to bring to the planning department. Apparently, they are in charge of supplies. If there is no signature from the boss, they deny my request. It is just like in the old days, when I had to go to the concierge with a letter from my parents to call in sick at school... Honestly, sometimes I just put my own name and signature on it myself. I don't even think they pay close attention to the memo: as long as there is one with a signature on it, they'll approve."

Nelson goes on: "If everything is fine, they grab the gloves from the pantry. But the pantry is full of stuff we don't need, and what we need is always out of stock. So then they must place an order. And because they accumulate the orders until they have enough to place a large order without shipping costs, I receive my new gloves two weeks later if I'm unlucky."

I look at Paul questioningly. He responds: "Ronald, this is the process we introduced last year when you told us to save costs. A target was introduced, and we can only achieve it by keeping the stock supply small. The responsibility for ordering supplies lies with the manager, which is why Thom has to give permission. Often things 'disappeared' from the pantry during that period. That's why at one point we've locked the room."

I can hardly believe what I hear. The shipping costs may have gone down, but we have gained a lot of hidden costs in return. I don't even want to start thinking about the impact it has on our delivery time.

This can't be true. Those gloves cost ten pounds, maybe twenty? But a professional who has to schedule a meeting, and then has to chase down planning to get his new gloves, and in the meantime can't do his job properly, resulting in a delay for the customer—what would that cost? My face grows red with shame. But I keep calm and ask inquisitively: "How would you prefer it to work?"

Nelson replies: "Well, just like we did with my previous boss. I went to the pantry and grabbed what I needed. And when if we were almost out of supplies, I simply ordered a bunch of new things online. They would arrive the next day. Just like I would do at home. The only difference is that I paid with the business credit card."

Nelson continues: "But that's not all. The worst thing is time tracking. If I don't punch in my time card exactly at 8:00 a.m., wages will be withheld."

Now he is starting to sound like he is complaining. I ask critically: "What is wrong with that? Isn't it normal to agree to arrive at work on time?"

Nelson looks at me, annoyed: "Yes, boss. But it happens quite often that at the end of the day I have almost finished with a kitchen that has to be taken for installation the next day. I then prefer to continue working late. That's not only nice for me but mainly for the customer, you know? I don't need additional overtime pay; I would be fine with compensating the hours at a later, quieter moment. But if I don't punch in exactly on time, I will get fined for it. So at 4:30 p.m., I just stop caring about the work and peace out for the day. Oh, yeah, you know what's even worse? When I arrive at the time clock, already four people are lined up because everyone wants to leave exactly on time."

"Thom, what do you think of this?" I say urgently.

Thom shrugs his shoulders and looks at Paul: "Well, you know, our smart guys in the planning departments send us a very precise schedule from 8:00 a.m. to 4:30 p.m. with a detailed description of what people have to do during each half hour. I have already mentioned that to you, Paul, that this is inconvenient that we have absolutely no slack in our planning. If something goes wrong, then the entire schedule runs into the ground. A small setback in the morning can sometimes result in four fewer kitchens being finished that day."

Paul responds defensively: "If they are not finished on time, the carpenter probably made a mistake somewhere, right? I always see them drinking coffee and having a smoke outside. Apparently, there is plenty of time for that! Do we really have to start paying them overtime? There is also time to wait fifteen minutes in advance at the time clock!"

Nelson responds unashamedly: "It seems like you only hired me as a 'resource.'" He makes a gesture of quotation marks with his fingers in the air. "But you seem to forget that I am a person, a craftsman who is very good at his job. I believe it would be much better if I would be allowed to discuss amongst my colleagues what should happen when exactly. If there is a problem, we will talk about how we can solve it, so that we can get it done on time for the customer."

I am seriously shocked by what I hear. I conclude the conversation: "Nelson, thank you for raising this and being honest with us. This really helps greatly to improve our company, step by step!"

Why are my managers micromanaging? This reminds me of what Edwin said. If you want to gain speed, you must have a lightweight organization that harnesses the intelligence of everyone. Employees who act without asking permission. We have hired smart people, so why should we tell them what to do?

I plan to discuss it with Emily in the evening. But as soon as I get home, I see that she is busy studying for her final exam of the course. Fortunately, she no longer seems angry. We decide not to cook and order pizza and pasta delivery. We devour the pizza and pasta in its entirety. Emily seems to eat even more than I do.

Faster Decisions

Tuesday

The next morning, I discuss with my management team what we have heard from Nelson. I ask Thom how he experienced it. He responds with disdain: "It's true what Nelson said. But I am afraid that if we remove the rules, we will no longer be in control. You know, I am responsible for the targets being met. I am judged if things go wrong so I think it is important to know exactly who is doing what and how money is spent."

I respond firmly, "I understand, Thom. But our world has really changed. We simply have to take more risk; otherwise, we will never go faster. And that we can't afford. Every kitchen we give away for free is much more expensive than that one pair of gloves that someone takes home by accident or on purpose. Paying overtime or being flexible with working hours costs a lot less than a kitchen that is installed too late. Penny wise, pound foolish. If we don't do anything about it, we'll soon be out of a job. I'll be the first one to be fired. Do you understand?"

My argument seems to be received well. Except with Paul. He responds: "Yes, but do you remember what Nelson proposed? He proposed to completely get rid of the planning. Remember when we introduced centralized planning, we gained enormous efficiency. We can't simply hand it over to the people, can we? They don't oversee the situation. In fact,

I even wonder if they can bear the responsibility. You know, I went to university, but they..."

I finish his sentence: "They are just stupid workers?" Paul sighs deeply.

I continue: "It has also made me realize something else. It sounds like your team members are bursting with good ideas about how we can go faster, but nothing is done with it. And at some point, people will stop mentioning their ideas and disengage. Do you recognize this?"

Laura responds: "Yes, but they often come up with things where they say 'trust us, just leave it to us, let us decide,' and I find that difficult. If everyone just does whatever they want, it'll be chaos."

Thom agrees: "Exactly. In order for a team to function properly, you need a boss who gives direction and keeps the pressure on."

I react: "If we want to get out of this shitty situation, we have to do exactly what they ask for, Laura. We have to change our attitude. This change is not just a change in the way we work. I am slowly beginning to realize this. This change is a different way of thinking, and that starts with us—if we don't believe that our people have the best intentions for the company, then that mainly says something about ourselves; after all, why did we hire these people in the first place? They are all professionals. People must be given the trust that they can improve their department themselves because if we hold that responsibility with us, they will continue to lean back."

Laura nods, "Hmm, that sounds reasonable. But how do we do that?"

Wilma reacts enthusiastically: "Well, I tried something last week, which worked pretty well. During the Friday session, I asked everyone in the team to write down one idea on a Post-it we could try to go faster. They really proposed dull things that I didn't believe would improve our way of working. For example, they wanted coat hooks in the toilets. And they suggested purchasing an additional coffee machine because there are always queues. But then I thought: maybe I shouldn't shut down their ideas this time. So I kept my mouth shut and asked if they wanted to vote for the best idea. They all looked at me, in disbelief I think, expecting me to knock their ideas down. To my surprise, they chose that extra coffee machine!"

The group is on the edge of their seats as they deeply listen to Wilma speak. She continues: "Such a fully automatic coffee machine isn't cheap, of course, but I bought one the same day. It cost a few hundred pounds, and I just paid it myself for the sake of quick action. And indeed, during the week, I saw more and more happy faces because the lines were almost gone. If I had suggested this myself, it would never have worked. But now they came up with it themselves, and it worked! By the way, can I expense that coffee machine?"

I respond enthusiastically: "That's awesome, Wilma. And of course, you can expense it. Okay, team, I have a proposal. Why don't we do the following every Friday: you let your teams vote for the best idea, and, whatever they come up with, you accept that idea and agree. If it goes wrong, we will reverse the decision, and I will not blame you for that. Does anyone object to that?"

Laura reacts skeptically: "Yes, but what if they only want to start at 11:00 a.m. and want to go home at 4:00 p.m.?"

Wilma squeezes her eyes and responds: "I highly doubt they would do that. They are not toddlers, are they?"

I respond: "And even if they do, then you just try it for a week and evaluate with them at the end of the week what the effect was. If you don't try, then you don't know, do you?

And if working fewer hours indeed leads to more speed and results, then it's fine, isn't it?"

Thom is not convinced and says: "But what if they want to buy a very expensive new machine?"

I take a moment to think. "I can see your point," I respond. I grab from my bag the page I received yesterday. I read it quickly: most decisions are reversible. Strive for a decision that is "safe to try" and learn from the result. Ah!

I say: "That is a decision with potentially major consequences that can't simply be reversed. I propose we will continue to make such decisions in our management team, but all reversible decisions, you just let them go ahead with it. How does that sound? Do you think it's safe to try, say, for a month? Again, if it goes wrong, I promise it won't affect your performance review."

Everyone nods in agreement. "Okay, we have half an hour left. What's the next agenda item?" We have never made a joint decision so quickly. This feels like progress.

I state that I intend to be on the production floor more often and I encourage my managers to do the same. In the days that follow, I cancel my morning meetings and instead talk to as many people as possible in the workplace. I help people in every department. I assist with making offers, answering our customers' questions, and even producing and installing a kitchen. And I ask questions, many questions. What they all tell me...it's amazing. Countless small and large things that we can improve very easily. People light up, feel that they are heard, and I have never had so much fun.

We are fixing the things Nelson brought up. For example, we decided to disconnect the time clock and the wage payments for the time being, so that people can determine their own working hours. We are also doing an experiment in which the pantry (where the gloves are stored) is open to everyone, and the stock can be managed by the workers themselves. The effect of all those little improvements is immediately visible in our delivery time, which quickly drops from ten weeks to eight weeks.

∅

That evening Emily hints at the fact that she thinks it's time to have a baby after her exams are done. I answer that that is really an irreversible decision and that we, therefore, have to think carefully about it. Emily is irritated by my response. In recent months, she couldn't think about anything else, she says. It bothers her that she is apparently alone in this. When I inquire more, I discover that she has made moves already. She even already has bought a few sets of baby clothes when she was shopping with her sister. She kept the clothes with her sister and brother-in-law for now.

I find it all rather premature, but if it makes her happy, fine. I decide not to ask more about it because the topic often ends in a fight, and I can't handle that right now. And apparently, that's fine with Emily as well, since she changed the subject herself.

PART FIVE

Final Lap

To the Factory

Early October – average delivery time: eight weeks

At 6:30 a.m., I'm already in my car on my way to the office. I'm surprised that even at this time there is traffic. When I arrive, I meet Nelson, Wilma, and Laura in the parking lot. They step in my car.

Today we're driving up to Milton Keynes to visit the factory of the Faster Racing Formula 1 team.

Last week Paul called me. A customer offered him tickets for a very exclusive factory tour at Faster Racing, which is only organized twice a year and usually costs 500 pounds per person. But due to circumstances, four tickets suddenly became available, and he wanted to give them to us as a thank you for our good service.

I didn't need long to think about it and immediately confirmed. Unfortunately, Paul couldn't come; he is visiting the World Kitchen Expo in the US this week. I proposed it to Laura and Wilma, and they were immediately enthusiastic. Thom didn't like it but he suggested to invite Nelson from production instead. I liked that idea, given that Nelson really helped us a lot and he is a positive example in our organization.

My GPS guides us into an industrial area. Suddenly we see a huge building with a large "Faster Racing" sign on the outside. We park the car and go inside. There we meet the rest of the tour group. Another ten or so others. Most of them are completely crazy about Formula 1. Half of them even wear clothing from the Faster Racing team.

A hostess receives us: "Hello, everyone, and welcome to the entrance of our factory. My name is Amy. I will guide you today. The first thing you see here is our prize cabinet." She points to a glass wall, floor to ceiling certainly ten meters high, which is full of trophies from several races.

"Obviously, we are very proud of our achievements. But another reason to place this prize cabinet at the entrance is that it reminds everyone of the purpose of the work we're doing here. As an organization, we have one clear goal: winning races and championships. Everything is geared towards that goal. Close to a thousand people work here, but together we are one big team. A clear and shared goal helps to strengthen our one team mindset."

Laura nudges me and whispers: "Maybe we should also define one shared goal. Something with delivery time perhaps?" I nod and then turn my attention back to Amy.

"After every race weekend, we know where we stand, compared to that goal and the competition. I consider that a luxury. In my previous job, I worked for a large company. It was not at all clear what the purpose of my work was and how I could contribute. Making our shareholders rich also wasn't really a goal that energized me. Here, at Faster Racing, it is completely different. Everyone knows exactly how their work contributes to the end result, and you can see the effect very quickly."

We follow Amy into a meeting room. It is more like an aquarium, with glass walls reaching from the floor to the ceiling. The view is impressive: we can see the factory hall. Below us are a couple of mechanics working on a Formula 1 car. What stands out most is how sterile and pristine the interior is. White walls and a white cast floor. The floor is clean, and tools are neatly stored in drawers. No sight of oil stains or other dirt.

"That's a nice production floor; isn't it, Nelson?" says Wilma.

"You can say that again. I'd love to set up our production floor like this," Nelson responds enthusiastically.

Amy: "You are right on time; they're just starting their pit stop rehearsal." I see a group of mechanics put on helmets and gloves. One of them climbs in a car. As soon as everyone is ready, he drives towards the group, after which the team changes tires within a second or two, just like on the circuit. Nelson and Laura are visibly impressed.

Amy continues: "This team practices every morning and evening, ten times. Only with this discipline can they achieve perfection. Doing pit stops is not their full-time job. One guy is an IT engineer, someone else is responsible for goods transport, and a number of them are mechanics. Working in the pit stop team is a role that they take on alongside their normal work. We don't value fixed job titles that much. We remain flexible if we identify roles that can change regularly. You also may have noticed: the car they use for practice is electric, which saves a lot of noise and exhaust fumes. Feel free to grab a drink from the kitchen, next to this meeting room. When you are all set, I'll tell you more about our team."

Some of the other people in the tour look surprised when they see Nelson and Wilma scrutinize the kitchen before they even grab a drink: "What brand of kitchen is this, Nelson?" asks Wilma.

Nelson responds: "Well, this is certainly not a Kitchen Quick, because we would finish these seams a little tighter. The sink is nice, I think; the composite kitchen top flows perfectly into the basin."

After everyone grabs a drink and gets back in the conference room, Amy takes us through the production process. A dazzling list of teams is discussed: design, machine shop, aero performance, 3D printing, carbon fiber processing, paint, gearbox, wheel suspension, hydraulics, drivetrain, brakes, electronics, assembly, wind tunnel testing, stress testing, inspection and compliance testing, logistics, data analysis, and strategy. Wow, I knew it was large, but I didn't expect it to be so grandiose.

Amy says: "We produce around 80 percent of the parts of the cars ourselves. Ultimately, all this work must come together as one super-fast car. Collaboration between the teams is essential, as you understand. That is why we only hire people who are real team players. We find that more important than hiring the best 'hard skills.' If someone is not the very best, we can often teach them those skills. But it's very difficult to change self-centered people to work together."

Nelson asks: "Do you have a planning team that coordinates the activities of each department?"

Amy answers: "Great question! No, the teams constantly coordinate amongst each other. Central planning would be too slow for us. Instead, we work with a fixed rhythm. Every morning and evening, delegates from the teams meet in a short stand-up meeting to discuss the state of affairs and resolve any problems or dependencies. Almost all communication happens face-to-face; we rarely use email internally." I could see the glow on Nelson's face.

I ask: "Alright, but what if one of the teams has a delay in delivery? Then you still want to know the impact on the overall planning, right?"

Amy: "All information is shared transparently between the teams. We have software which visualizes the status of components. So we don't have to coordinate that centrally, because it is automated. It happens quite often that a delay happens and one team has to wait for another team. But people won't complain about that; everyone assumes that their colleagues are doing their utmost to put the very latest innovations in the new part. We don't point fingers, even if that sometimes means working in the evening because another team has caused a delay. If your car is finished a few days before the race, then you have missed the opportunity to innovate a few days!"

We follow Amy into the factory. First of all, we pass the Race Simulator. This looks like a kind of computer game. Through a window, I see someone using the steering wheel in the cockpit of a Formula 1 car. A giant curved screen around him shows a race circuit. The car even moves up and down in the corners. I'd love to have this game console at home! Suddenly I notice that it is Mark who is sitting behind the wheel.

Amy explains that all new parts are first designed on the computer. They are then tested by the computer in a kind of virtual wind tunnel, which they call Computational Fluid Dynamics. The approved parts are then screwed onto the car virtually. The computer model of the simulator is so advanced that, by driving a few laps, Mark can sense whether the new part is indeed an improvement, while the part actually only exists virtually. Pretty bizarre!

The next destination is the 3D print shop. Amy explains that these machines can produce a new part very quickly and precisely. These parts are then tested in a real wind tunnel. Only when they seem an improvement, do they create the real parts, usually from lightweight carbon fiber.

We can peek through a window, where we see about ten men and women in protective clothing making the molds for the carbon fiber parts. To prevent minuscule deviations, their room has an airlock and a special air treatment system to make the room dust-free and keep it at a constant temperature. The parts are then evacuated and baked in an autoclave: a high-pressure oven. The pressure is built to up to 7 bar. When a part is ready, it is inspected by means of ultrasonic sound. Impressive!

Wilma asks: "How long does it take in total to make a new front wing?"

Amy: "The simple answer is: as quickly as possible and faster than the competition! Thanks to all improvements, all cars become on average two seconds per lap faster, during the racing season. We are making more than 750 large and smaller adjustments per week. So, the faster we can create a part, the better. That is why we automate all the repetitive work. Some parts can even be made ready for dispatch within twenty-four hours: design, simulation, production, and testing. Sometimes we even ship improved parts to the circuit as late as Friday night. This allows them to assemble them on the car on Saturday morning, just in time for the last free practice session and qualifying."

We continue walking through the machine shop. A large hall with computer-controlled metal cutting machines. Nelson is very impressed: "Wow, those devices cost at least 600,000 pounds each. And I count about fifteen of them." It occurs to me that everyone here has access to the best possible tools. And that producing a Formula 1 car is really expensive.

At the end of a long corridor, we see a room with mirrored windows. The kind of glass that you can look into from one side, but you see yourself from the other side. I think they call that "interview glass" because they use it at the police station for their interrogation rooms. We are not allowed to go in there. Amy says that this is where they are working on innovations for the car of the next season. Halfway through the season, roughly a third of the people and resources are made available to work on larger innovations for next season. It allows them to think calmly, away from the fast pace of incremental innovation for the short-term.

Amy says the team has a budget of around 350 million pounds a year. And at the end of the year, they have spent almost every penny on making the car faster. People have a decent salary, and there are bonuses, but no profits are made. The sponsors only invest money for marketing and increased brand awareness.

We also get to see the remote garage: the room where, during the race, dozens of people closely monitor real-time sensors on the car and help make decisions about the racing strategy. It looks like a NASA mission control room where they monitor the rocket launches. In front of the room, there is a wall covered by a huge screen, which shows all kinds of graphs. Behind the screen are dozens of workplaces with their own computer screens and microphones. It occurs to me that at the circuit, I heard this team talking when listening to what was being said on the headphones. It's interesting to see it in real life now as well.

Before we go back home, I visit the toilet. Even here I get inspired.

There is a saying on the wall: "*People who say it can't be done, should not interrupt those who are doing it!*"

Insomnia

Two weeks later – average delivery time: six weeks

I can't fall asleep that night. My mind is still racing. We've made a lot of progress in the past period. Due to several improvements that the teams suggested, we are speeding up. Thom eventually provided two carpenters to make all the blueprints. They do that as soon as possible after the order has been placed. The result: no more surprises during the installation of the kitchen. Also, for a few days, we completely assemble the kitchen on our production floor before loading it on the bus. At first, this may seem like extra work, but it also means that we can fix small issues immediately.

All these experiments have decreased our delivery time significantly, to now only six weeks. But progress has stalled. What else can I do to reach two weeks?

I often listen to a podcast to help me fall asleep. I open the app and see the available episodes. Cool! The Formula 1 podcast has a new episode with team boss Edwin! Now I'm sure I won't fall asleep. I put my earbuds in and listen to the interview. The interviewer asks: "Edwin, can you tell something about your management style?"

I prick up my ears and turn up the volume: "It is actually quite simple," Edwin replies. "I leave most of it to my people. We employ professionals and I expect them to make their own decisions. People are perfectly capable to take responsibility for their life and family at home. Why wouldn't they be able to do that at work? Do you ask your manager for permission when you want to buy a house? Of course not. Moreover, your people usually are more knowledgeable than you. I often hear business managers complain that they give their people responsibility, but that they don't dare to make decisions. I then tell them that it is their own fault. Of course they don't want to hear that. You simply can't give responsibility; you have to make sure people want to and can take responsibility. And if that doesn't happen, then apparently you're not doing your job properly."

The interviewer, somewhat confused, asks: "That sounds very easy, but how do you put that into practice?" I turn on my bedside lamp and start taking notes on my notepad. Emily grumbles. She turns her back to the light.

Edwin answers the question patiently: "If you treat people like adults, they also behave like adults. But if you continue to make decisions for your people as a manager, then they will never do it themselves. Some colleagues in our team also ask me sometimes for permission, especially the newer colleagues. They soon find out that I always ask the same question: 'If we do what you propose, will it make the car go faster?' If the answer is 'yes' then my answer is always 'just do it.' That's the only thing that matters. That's what we do it for. If you keep doing that consistently, they'll stop asking you at some point, because they already know what you're going to say."

The interviewer asks: "But how do you ensure that they make the right decisions?"

Edwin: "Success must be clearly defined. Because if the desired outcome is not clearly defined, how can you be successful? And if that is clear, then you can leave it to the people themselves. When they have all the information, they also make the right decisions. They know what they are doing it for. Therefore, in our team, all information is available to everyone. This way our people can make their own decisions as if they were the CEO of the team. Even when a lot of money is involved. It is also nice because it means I don't have to sit in meetings all day. I just walk around during the day and have a chat here and there. I always learn more from that than sitting in a meeting room looking at a report!"

What wonderful insights again. I write them down one by one. It reminds me of a documentary I saw on the BBC about self-management, which Emily recently wanted to see for her schoolwork. The episode highlighted organizations without managers: there the people who do the work also manage the company. The traditional work of managers is still there but was distributed in a different way.

Yes, I now know what I have to do next. I turn off the light and fall asleep quickly.

Common Sense

The end of October, Monday morning, weekstart — average delivery time: five weeks

he canteen is packed with people today. Since we've started to ask teams for improvements, the atmosphere in the company has become much more positive. This is noticeable during the weekstart. I'm standing in the back of the room myself and have a hard time seeing the podium. Last week we decided to rotate the facilitation of the weekstart within our management team.

Laura is on stage and says: "Good morning, everyone. I hope you had a good weekend!" The room reacts enthusiastically: "Mooorning!" Laura continues: "I will first update you on the latest metrics. Of course, I will start with the delivery time. It is going down rapidly and is now only at five weeks. Customer satisfaction is up from 6.5/10 to 7/10 last week." People cheer.

Laura continues: "Okay, now I would like to invite the production team to say a few words." Nelson and another colleague climb on stage. I notice that they both have a pencil behind their ears; pretty typical. Did they decide to coordinate their outfits beforehand? Nelson appears a lot happier these days. Laura: "We are curious: what mistakes did you make last week, what did you learn from them, and what improvement will you try this week?"

Nelson proudly says: "For years our plywood occasionally had small cracks in it. Sometimes we only saw that during or after sawing. When that happened, we would simply pick up a new piece of plywood from the stock and start over. Before, we had plenty of time to do that, but now we can no longer afford it. This week we called the supplier and asked them to come over so we could show them the problem. It was a surprise to them. They suspect it happens because they often load the plates into their cold trucks when they are still warm. They promised they would fix this problem, and we made some agreements about the minimum quality level of their deliveries. In the coming period, we will monitor whether things are indeed improving. We expect this will save us a lot of time."

The other teams also share their lessons and experiments one by one. Laura is ready to end the gathering: "Is there anyone else who wants to say something before we close the session?"

I raise my hand and say: "Yes, I would like to say something."

I squeeze myself through the crowd. Once at the front I say: "Hello, everyone. I want to say that I am very proud of your efforts and the improvements we are making. I would like to go one step further. Up until now, you often expect me or your manager to make decisions. What I would like from now on is that you decide more things yourself. Do you have an improvement idea that results in the kitchen being delivered to the customer faster, is your idea "safe to try" and is it in the best interest of the company or the customer? Then use your common sense and no longer wait for me or one of the other managers to approve the idea. Instead, act as if you already have permission. In the worst case, you can always say sorry afterward. If the outside world requires a signature from management, then come to me. I will sign everything, blindly!"

My managers look at me in surprise. Hmm, maybe I was too impulsive again and I should have discussed this with them first. But not long after, Wilma gives me a wink and Laura shows me a thumbs up. They seem to understand what I am trying to do.

At least that's what I think.

Automate

The weeks after my impulsive announcement were a bit chaotic. A lot went wrong, but we learned a lot from it. For example, the production team decided to buy a new fully automatic sawing machine. An investment of over 100,000 pounds! They've always wanted a new sawing machine, but Thom never permitted it. They clearly remembered my remark that it is better to say sorry afterward than to ask for permission beforehand.

They had asked a salesman to visit us on a day when Thom wasn't in the office. They immediately placed the order for the machine. I didn't expect that something like this would happen. Thom was furious when he discovered what happened. First, he scolded his whole team, then he called the supplier to cancel the order. But that wasn't possible. Apparently, my signature was on the order. I had signed it blindly. Thom was devilish. He threatened to fire his entire team. Soon all his people were standing furious at my desk, including Nelson. I quickly discovered that he was the driving force behind all this.

I asked Thom to come into my office. The conversation was very difficult and lasted a long time. Thom took it very personally and remained emotional. He kept hammering at his most important point: who is really in charge of the department? He or Nelson? The conversation just kept going in a circle. At one point, Thom even shouted: "He out or I out!" In the end, I had to make it clear to him that this was not an option. We have to work it out together as a team, and conflicts are part of that.

And it was true, the machine immediately caused enormous acceleration. Many manual operations can now be performed fully automatically, just like at the racing team's factory. Nelson had paid close attention during the visit. The machine is not only faster but also much less prone to errors. Nelson showed me and Thom a calculation, which showed we could earn back the investment within six months. Thom finally had to reluctantly agree with him. Then Nelson indicated that he wanted to purchase three additional machines. This would double our capacity, and it would result in a speed increase of at least a week.

Thom could not take the idea of buying three more of these expensive machines. He turned pale, stood up, and left the room. I tried to find him later, but he was nowhere to be found. The receptionist said he had reported sick and went home.

I learned through the company doctor that Thom was burned out from work. The following week I agreed with Thom and the doctor that it would be best if he would really take a long break, instead of returning too soon. He had a hard time letting go, which tore him apart. Thom has been working at our company for so long. He deserves a role that suits him and makes him happy. When he feels better, we will look for a solution together. I'm sure we can work it out.

For a moment, I thought about having Nelson temporarily fill the position of Thom. But that turned out not to be necessary at all. The production and placement teams decided to continue working together as one team. Wilma could manage that fine, she said. Wilma is loved by her people, which helps a lot.

Combining the two teams helped reduce another two days lead time because apparently the placement team always conducted an extensive intake of the produced parts. It's a quality check that was also conducted right before by the production team. This is duplicate work that we can now stop doing.

Our delivery time keeps going down by the way! Thanks to the four new fully automatic sawing and milling machines, we're currently at three weeks. In some cases, we even manage to do it within two weeks, if everything goes well and the kitchen is basic. What a difference with where we came from. I didn't think this was possible.

Into the Gravel

End of November — average delivery time: three weeks

Today I decided to go home in the early afternoon. Nowadays the factory mostly runs itself. I notice I'm starting to get more free time. Finally! After lunch, I turn off my computer and walk out of my room. On the way down I call my favorite Michelin starred restaurant and ask if there is any chance of an available table. They are actually fully booked, but we're allowed to sit in the kitchen at the chef's table that just came available. I decide to surprise Emily tonight.

As soon as I walk into the living room, I take a seat on the couch next to Emily. Finally, I feel the peace to start the conversation about children. I place my hand on her leg and say, "Sweetheart, I'd like to discuss something with you."

She responds, "Oh, what's on your mind?"

"Well, we've talked about it before, but I really think we should wait a few more years before we have children. We still want to go to Australia, and you have been talking about a trip to Africa for years. I don't think we should combine that with children. And we are still young enough. We could easily delay this by three years. And it is also much better with your new degree. You're almost finished and you'll be able to use your new knowledge a few years to start your new career."

Emily frowns and says curtly: "No, Ronald. I see it differently. Delay always leads to cancellation. Everything in me says that we should no longer wait."

I get frustrated because she gives me no choice. In fact, she seems to have already decided. I respond: "I understand, but shouldn't we make this decision together? You cannot decide this on your own."

"I don't know, Ronald. If we wait, you're deciding for me, aren't you? I don't want to wait. I've waited long enough. You know that, right? And if you don't want children, then you need to tell me that very quickly!"

"Yes, I know, but you also know that living in New York is one of my dreams. How can we do that when we have a child?"

Emily gets up and starts shouting: "Stop it! I've always sacrificed myself for your career. I moved with you to this hell hole. And now I want you to do this for me, but again you only think about yourself. You just don't grant me my happiness!"

She walks out of the living room and weeps up the stairs to the bedroom. After a while, I want to ask how she's doing, but it's too late. She has decided. As soon as she returns to the living room, she carries a large weekend bag over her shoulder.

She says curtly: "I'm going to stay with my sister for a few days. I have to think very carefully, Ronald. Not about children, but about us!" She walks through the living room to the front door. I hear the door slam into the lock.

I had not seen this coming at all. The work situation finally starts to clear up, but now it is a mess at home. Sighing, I pour a glass of cognac and drink it in one go.

Is this what I want? Is this all worth it?

Despair

While I am still thinking about what just happened with Emily, my phone rings. I don't recognize the number. I decline the call twice, but it keeps calling back. I pick up, irritated. It is Hank. He sounds confused or drunk. But he also sounds a bit panicky. He asks me to come to a pub called Ye Olde Hook, in the center of London. I have not been there for a long time. I know it from when I was still a student, a long time ago.

I see Hank's red convertible parked in front of the cafe. I walk inside. The bartender is drying a glass. He sees me looking around and apparently notices that I'm worried. "You're probably here for him?" He nods to a corner in the back of the pub where Hank sits alone at a table behind a glass of whisky. At first, I don't recognize him. He wears a black leather jacket and looks like he hasn't shaved for a month. He has very puffy eyes as if he has not slept for quite a while. I walk over to him and smell that he also hasn't showered for quite a while. It is a smell of sweat and alcohol that fits a homeless person. It doesn't fit Hank. This is Mr. Rapid, the Kitchen Cowboy. A proud, flamboyant man. There is not much of that left.

I order two cups of coffee and sit opposite him. On the table, I see his thick leather wallet and his car keys. It is clear to me that he had too much to drink to be able to drive. I grab his keys and put them in my pocket. Hank does not even protest. I touch his shoulder: "Hey, Hank, I don't know you this way. What is the matter?"

He looks at me emotionally and explains that he is on the brink of personal bankruptcy. He is out of money. We have been giving away kitchens for free for almost half a year now because we can't place them within two weeks. Although the delivery time is becoming shorter and shorter, many customers still get their kitchen for free.

I can feel the ground fall out from underneath my feet. How could I be so stupid? How is it possible that I have lost track of finances? But at the same time, Hank has always been in control of the financial side of things. He tells me he has kept depositing his personal money into the account, which has enabled us to pay our bills. And he has often said he had deep pockets. He is a multi-millionaire, right? Not anymore. In front of me sits a defeated man. A man who is in despair.

Hank grabs me and says: "You are the only one who can still steer us out of this, Ronnie. After all, you have already taken the biggest steps. Bring it back to two weeks. You are almost there! Then all the problems are solved. Can I count on you?"

I feel sorry for him. And I do feel responsible for the current situation. It even seems like it gives me energy. I look him directly in the eyes and also grab his shoulders. I respond in the affirmative: "Of course, Hank. You can count on me. I'm going to do my very best! We are going to achieve this together. We are almost there!"

The bartender comes running with the two cups of coffee. I knock back mine and force Hank to drink his. Then I quickly pay and guide Hank to my car. I drop him off at home. He'll have to pick up his car tomorrow.

PART SIX

Finish Line

Overtaking

As I drive back home, all kinds of thoughts go through my mind. It is all very paradoxical. On the one hand, the company has never run so well in terms of delivery time. At the same time, we have never been so close to bankruptcy. Right when I have more time to spend at home with Emily, and right when I get used to the idea of getting kids, our relationship is at an all-time low and she is with her sister.

What now? I decide to give Emily some space. Everything I say or do right now will probably make it worse. I phone my brother-in-law, her sister's husband. He indicates that it is not too bad and that he thinks Emily isn't that angry anymore. He recommends that I call her that evening and also says something about women and pregnancy. I am so relieved she has calmed down that I don't pay attention to what he says.

Then I look for Edwin's phone number, the Formula 1 team boss. I prepare myself for recording a voicemail, while he suddenly answers: "Hello, this is Edwin."

Out of enthusiasm, I start talking: "Hey, hello! This is Ronald Park. How nice to talk to you now. I wasn't able to catch you before. We met during the race in Belgium, do you remember? By the way, thanks so much for taking the time to send me some tips, that really helped!"

"You are welcome. But I have no idea what you are talking about. Ronald, did you say? Oh yeah, I remember now. You are the kitchen guy of Francorchamps!?" In the background, I hear racing cars passing by.

"Yes indeed! You then gave me some advice on how we can speed up. I started applying those ideas. Involving people, making it safe to learn from mistakes, making decisions faster, freeing up time every week to learn and reflect, and so on. Every department is really good at speeding up, but now we still have to make a leap. We have managed to reduce the delivery time from sixteen weeks to three weeks. That's great, but we urgently have to take another week off. Do you have any ideas?"

Edwin responds as if I'm asking a stupid question: "What I remember from our conversation is that you had already managed to once do it in two weeks, right? Is that correct? Why was it possible then?"

I respond as if he gave a stupid answer: "Yes, you mean that kitchen for the princess? Yeah, that's right, but that's a whole different story. It was a unique circumstance."

Edwin says resolutely: "Nothing is a unique circumstance. Or everything is one. In that lies your solution. Our very best pit stop forms the basis for all pit stops. We learn from it how to succeed. We will try to do it more often. You have already proven you can do it in two weeks. That's not much different from our situation. It makes no sense to have the fastest gearbox in the world when the rest of the car is crap."

I have no clue what he is talking about and respond: "Sorry, but I don't follow you. What is the link between a gearbox and a kitchen?"

In the background, another car rushes by with a deafening noise. Edwin raises his voice: "Stop thinking in departments! They don't matter! It is about what one does and what you can do, not about which department you're from! Create a small team that delivers results from the beginning to the end. Just like we do." He waits for a few more cars to pass and then continues: "It's just like a pit stop. One operates the front jack, the other unscrews the left rear tire, yet another puts the wheel on it, and so on. They are all different disciplines, but at the same time they are working on one result for which they are jointly responsible."

Now I'm starting to understand, I think. I try to imagine how long a pit stop would take if a car first receives a new right front tire and then has to drive to the next pit box for the left front tire. And then, in a bad case, first has to wait until it is his turn. Duh! Of course that doesn't work. And, of course, that is way too slow.

Edwin asks, "Hey, are you still there?"

I say: "Yeah, apologies, I had to let it sink in for a moment. So you propose to create one team that handles an entire kitchen, from start to finish? From the moment of sale to placement? But that is not possible at all!"

Edwin, clearly irritated, says in a sarcastic tone: "Yes, that's always what they say, 'that won't work for us.' Well, if you don't try, then you will never know! It is just like working out. When you go to the gym for the first time you will get muscle strain. You would never say 'working out doesn't work for me because it gives me muscle strain,' would you? Hey, uh, I have to go now. Don't be afraid. You can do it! Just do it!" He hangs up on me.

I stare out the window of my car for about ten minutes. Suddenly I also think of that saying at Faster Racing: "People who say it cannot be done should not interrupt those who are doing it." Perhaps I am indeed stuck in thinking in impossibilities. What if we would just do it that way? If we would work in small teams that completely measure, build, and install a kitchen. Just like a pit stop. Could that be the solution?

Damn!! Placing kitchens like a pit stop! Then it really becomes 'Formula Kitchen'!

Pi

January – delivery time: one week!

When I suggested the idea of "pit stop teams" at the start of the week, not everyone was enthusiastic. They remembered the racing analogy from Hank's commercials, which had messed up the whole place. The production and placement departments were the first to support it. After all, they had been merging their teams for several weeks. They proudly said that they now enjoyed their work much more because they were working together for the customer. No "us versus them," they called it.

The remark about us versus them immediately reminded me of home.

For the first time in our relationship, Emily and I have truly gone through a considerable crisis. We were really opposed to each other on the subject of children. Especially when she found out that she had started taking her birth control pills too late. She suspected her increased appetite perhaps meant she was pregnant, and she didn't feel like she could share that with me. This turned out to be a false alarm, but my proposal to delay starting a family really had her doubt our entire relationship. We kept blaming each other. Luckily we gradually started to listen to each other more. I needed to listen more than she did, so I was extra conscientious about hearing her out. It was a good move for Emily to stay with her sister for a while because it soon became clear to us that we missed each other enormously. Due to the hustle and bustle of work and study, we hardly talked to each other anymore. We were no longer the team that we were for years, and that led to all sorts of misunderstandings.

At Christmas when we were at her parents' house, I was surprised when I heard Emily talk to her mother about children. They stood in the kitchen, just around the corner. I overheard the conversation without them noticing. She spoke openly with her mother about her own doubts as to whether she should start with children at all. Certainly now with her education and career switch. This was a revelation for me. I thought Emily was eager to get pregnant. But apparently, that wasn't completely true. A child would turn her life upside down, and she wasn't sure if she really wanted that. The fact that she had thought she was pregnant for a while had made her think a lot. I was completely surprised. She added: "I often argue with Ronald about it, but that's not so much about me wanting children now. It is mainly because he gives me the feeling that I am not allowed to give my input. He has already decided not to want them, and I have to accept that."

Back in the car, we had a very good conversation. The strange thing was that we actually feel the same way. In terms of children, it is fifty-fifty for both of us. We want them, but why now? Only the harder Emily tried to convince me to start, the harder I started to push back. Here, too, "action leads to reaction." This made it seem like she was completely advocating for having children and I was 100 percent against it. But we were basically on the same page. We have now decided that we will hold off for the moment. Time will probably give us the insight we are looking for.

Anyway, back to work and the pitstop teams. We first started with a few teams. It took a while before the teams were used to being responsible for everything themselves.

That responsibility was certainly not always taken in the beginning. For example, some customers were still referred to the customer service line. We also noticed within the team people were still sticking to their old roles: "Yes, but I am from placement, so I don't help produce the kitchen," for example.

But the more teams became accountable for the entire customer journey, the better it went. We even shortened delivery time to less than a week for our simple kitchens! The experiment then grew very quickly. More and more people wanted to participate. Now, two months later, we are tilting the entire organization. We virtually have no departments anymore; instead, we have twenty multidisciplinary "pit stop" teams of four team members. Each team does one kitchen at a time. And they really do everything themselves. From measuring up and planning, up to and including production and placement. This includes maintaining contact with the customer and ordering of materials and equipment.

Laura's customer service team has been discontinued because the teams arrange customer contact themselves. Paul's sales team that work in the showrooms now pick up the central telephone and transfer calls to the teams as quickly as possible. Laura and a number of other colleagues whose jobs became obsolete fortunately soon found other jobs, and we guided them in finding those.

Those pit stop teams, what does that look like in practice? Let me explain it to you. The customer visits our web store or goes to one of our physical showrooms to learn about our kitchens. We have stopped doing complicated negotiations. The customer simply chooses from three options, each with a fixed price: Budget, Normal, or Luxury. Everyone pays the same. People buy their kitchen without fuss.

Budget and Normal have a delivery time of one week. Luxury takes two weeks. The customer chooses the calendar week in which they want the kitchen delivered. Often customers don't need to have it that quickly. If we are allowed to choose the date, the customer will receive a discount. That allows us to absorb changes in demand.

The timeline of a Budget and Normal kitchen looks like this. As soon as it is the week of delivery, the "pit stop team" will visit you on Monday afternoon. They measure up the room, make a 3D blueprint with the customer, and let the customer pick all the details on the spot: which equipment, which materials, etc. We call it a "showroom at home." The whole team visits the customer's home together. This allows them to see everything themselves, and no handoffs needed. Any problems can be seen by everyone, immediately and on the spot. Each team member can offer ideas and solutions from their own expertise. This often results in very smart workarounds that nobody, including the customer, would have thought of.

That same afternoon, the entire team creates a plan for the client, together with the client, at their house. They discuss whether there are constraints and issues to be dealt with, for example, a neighbor who sleeps late in the morning, or plumbing that needs to be changed—it doesn't matter. It is solved and arranged on the spot by the people who do the work.

On Tuesday and Wednesday, the team works in the factory to saw and assemble the kitchen to specification. They also do that all together. Any changes to electricity or plumbing are also done during these two days. Sometimes by one of the team members or by a self-employed person the team decides to recruit for these kinds of jobs. On Thursday morning the team is back at the customer's doorstep to install the kitchen. They bring their bus, which has a sawing machine built-in. So if they did miss something on Monday, they have all the necessary tools to make changes on the spot. No more hassle or waiting for new cupboards if something doesn't fit. Some people are even advocating to produce the whole kitchen on-site. This would remove the need for a factory; a warehouse would be sufficient. But I think that is still a bit too ambitious.

On Friday morning, the team does the finishing touch. The best moment of the week comes a few hours later: they throw a small celebration, together with the customer! From the bus they bring in a large bouquet of flowers, grab a bottle of champagne, and an apple pie, which they proudly bake on the spot in the new kitchen. Only if the customer wants that of course.

Before the team goes home to enjoy the weekend, they sit down to reflect on the past week. They discuss points for improvement and they give each other feedback. They do that wherever they want. Sometimes at the customer's, sometimes they drive back to the factory, but there are also teams that do it along the highway at a roadside restaurant. Or alternatively at home with team members, followed by a joint meal. I don't really care, as long as they take the time to get better together by learning from doing.

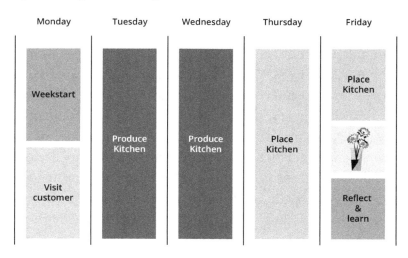

For Luxury kitchens, the weekly schedule almost looks the same, except the first week is dedicated to the production and the second is dedicated to placement.

On Monday morning everyone still comes together during the weekstart, in the canteen, at our factory. There we celebrate the successes and share the observations and lessons learned from the past week. This is crucial because teams can also learn from each other. The weekstart is very important for our learning.

If you take a good look at our weekly rhythm, you will see that the teams that build a Budget or Normal kitchen are only actually spending three and a half days on production and placement. One and a half days are spent on planning and learning. If we compress this even further, I think it should be possible to build and deliver within 72 hours. But I haven't told Hank that yet. I'm afraid he will immediately make a new commercial around that. And he'll probably exaggerate: a kitchen within a day. I can't dare to think about it.

I honestly think that customers would be interested in this. Maybe it will take a little longer to decide what you want for your kitchen, but once they decide, their kitchen could be installed the next day. Now, that would turn our market completely upside down!

Initially, there were some people who said it would not be efficient to spend a week with a whole team on one kitchen. But it doesn't matter, because it turns out to be extremely effective. And that is much more important.

We used to be super-efficient, but we hardly were able to get any kitchens out of the factory. Everyone was busy, but they actually got in each other's way. Only 60 percent of the staff actually touched a kitchen in their daily work. Everyone else was overhead and coordination. If you now look at the figures, you'll see it is actually much cheaper. Especially because there are fewer repairs, fewer errors, and decreased waiting time. Moreover, the teams now arrange a lot of things themselves that we used to have office staff or managers for.

I am proud of what we have achieved. Happy customers and results that the teams are proud of. Week after week. People have never been so happy in their work!

Thom is now back at work and works part-time. He discovered that he actually wasn't as happy in his role as manager and prefers to work with his hands. He joined a team that installs Luxury kitchens and he loves that. There are only a few managers left at our head office, including Wilma and Paul. They work in the background, facilitating, serving and supporting the teams.

And what do I do? Operationally, I am completely redundant. Everything arranges itself without me. Magnificent! I can now focus full time on the growth of our company.

I am no longer working *in* Kitchen Quick, but working *on* Kitchen Quick.

Finish

Hank asked me to meet him to look back on the past period. And honestly, I also really need that. I feel the need to tell him the truth about what he did. How could he do this, suddenly throwing a huge problem in our lap? It was totally irresponsible of him. Hank insisted that we shouldn't meet at the office but instead at his favorite golf club, on Saturday afternoon.

I typically don't have work meetings during the weekend. The crisis between Emily and me has made me realize that there is more to life than work alone. I'm surprised that in life we lean the hardest on the people you hold dearest, but in the process, we can neglect them completely. We agreed that working during weekends was off-limits. But this time I make an exception, after discussing it with Emily. She thought it was fine if I would cook a big meal tonight. I thought that was an excellent idea. Now that I have been home more often lately, I have developed myself as a reasonable hobby cook. And there are a few recipes for beautiful dishes that I would like to try.

Meeting Hank at his golf club is actually quite convenient since it is not far from our house. And today is a sunny day, a great day for cycling. It seems like winter has already passed. When I get on my bike, I see Emily waving me goodbye behind the window. It suddenly strikes me that she looks very different than usual. Much more happy and balanced. She really shines. A happy feeling takes hold of me. Could it be true...?

I wave back at her and give her a hand kiss while cycling away.

After half an hour of pedaling, I arrive at the golf club. I feel a bit uncomfortable on my mountain bike. The whole area is fenced off, and there is no separate pedestrian entrance. I arrive at a closed gate with a panel that looks like an intercom. I ride up to it on my bike and press a white button with a camera next to it. A tone sounds. After a few seconds, a strong white light turns on next to the camera and I hear an affluent voice: "Good afternoon?"

I realize that the camera probably shows the image of my buttocks on my saddle. A bit clumsily, I bow down and respond: "Yes, hello, I am coming for a meeting with Hank Rapid."

The voice responds: "Good afternoon, Mr. Park. Come on in. Mr. Rapid is expecting you."

The gate slides open. Behind it is a long driveway with trees. I see a huge clubhouse with a large parking lot at the end. I cycle across the road towards the clubhouse. On either side of the driveway, I see a handful of people working their golf balls and clubs. Almost all of them are men of Hank's age. Just over sixty. They look at me in surprise when they see me passing by on my bike.

When I arrive at the parking lot, I notice the huge amount of expensive cars. BMWs, Mercedes, Porsches, and Teslas. Even a red Ferrari. I park my bike right next to the clubhouse entrance. A bit around a corner, out of sight. When I lock my bike I see Hank waving at me from the terrace. "Hey, Ronnie, here!!" He looks neat; he wears a yellow polo shirt with bright green suspenders holding up his pants. No cowboy hat but a striped cap.

I walk over to him, and before I can say anything, he gives me a big hug. That is unlike Hank, to be so amicable. I say, somewhat perplexed: "Hi, Hank. How are you? You look a lot better than a few months ago in London. Then you looked like a homeless guy. And you also smelled like one!"

"Shh, shut up, hey, not everyone needs to know!" he whispers softly but urgently. We sit down. Hank immediately fires away and says: "Well, what shall we talk about?" Before I can respond, he signals the waiter and says: "Can I have a fresh juice? Do you want some too, Ronnie?"

I respond: "I'd like a cup of coffee, please."

I start off: "Well, Hank, what I want to talk about is how we prevent us from ending up in such a shitty situation again."

He frowns and says: "Shitty situation? What do you mean? Isn't it fantastic?! We have never had this much revenue. And our customers have never been so happy. Moreover, the people in the factory are more motivated than ever. Win-win-win!!"

I try to interrupt him in vain: "Yes, but..."

Hank immediately responds: "No 'buts.' You really did it, Ronnie. It is totally unnecessary to be depressed about it. Take a look at what you have achieved. Now tell me, how did you get the job done in the end?"

Hank's enthusiasm makes it difficult to stay angry for a long time. Little remains of my intention to be frank with him. He looks at me curiously, with big questioning eyes. I think back to the last months. A lot has happened indeed. As a kind of film, I see everything pass by. What a roller coaster! I could never have solved this without Edwin's inspiration and help.

This makes me reply: "It is actually a coincidence, Hank. I received VIP tickets for Formula 1. And that visit turned out to be worth gold! I met the team boss of a racing team there and I kept in touch with him. He gave me some important tips and insights. Later we also visited the factory, which we also learned a lot from!"

Hank starts to smile. "Shall I tell you a secret, Ronnie? I arranged that for you! Moreover, the other information also came from me, the page from the book. I also sent you the VIP tickets!" I look at him unbelievingly. What is this? Does Hank suddenly claim that he is behind this? He has a tendency to want to take credit for things, so I don't believe him.

I stay convinced of coincidence and reject the idea that he has anything to do with it and say, "Yeah, sure." Meanwhile, my face is in a frown that shows that I am not taking it seriously at all.

"No, Ronnie, really. For a while, I noticed the company was doing terribly. Everything was dormant and sleepy. It was mediocre, though everyone thought we were doing fine. But when I was traveling across China, I realized that the competition would be coming from there, soon. Something had to be done to wake up everything again. Including you. And if I would have given you those recommendations myself, you would never have accepted it. So I had to do something else to shake it loose. Hence the commercial, the VIP tickets, and the trip to the factory that I arranged with the help of Paul. This way you could discover it yourself. I knew you could do it!"

He continues: "And you really did great, but you didn't take the final step. Then I really had to get creative. I had to give you the idea that the end was really near and that I was almost bankrupt."

Before I can say anything, he continues: "I didn't shave and shower for a week. I smelled terrible. After that week I went to the pub. I drank three beers there and let the bartender place ten whiskys on the bill. Then I called you. I had to let you believe that everything was on fire. Only then would you take that final step. And only when the whole thing threatened to derail completely, you saw the solution. And you managed to get it done! I'm so proud of you!"

I am perplexed. Can this be true? It can't be, right? Did he fool me? I say: "Hank, what is this? You were almost bankrupt, right? Didn't you tell me that you spent all your money on free kitchens? We only had a few weeks left before it was too late, right?"

Hank looks at me with a smile and says: "No, Ronnie. Money did fly through the door, but that didn't bankrupt me. No worries, I have very deep pockets!" He then looks at his watch and says in a hurry: "Oh shit! Is it this late already? I have to go now because my tee time is in ten minutes and I have to warm up first."

He stands up and gives me a firm hand. He pulls me up to hug me again. What has gotten into him? He puts his arms on my shoulders again and looks me in the eye. Just like in that pub in London. He says: "Thanks again for all your hard work, Ronnie. You are the best managing director I could ever have wished for. And by the way, the notary will call you this week. Yesterday I signed over 25 percent of the shares in Kitchen Quick. They are yours now. We'll talk about that later."

Before I can respond, he walks around the corner and has disappeared. I am left behind, bewildered. I take a sip of my coffee and think about what he said. Does Hank have a link with Formula 1? And now suddenly he gives me shares? A quarter of the company? I'm stunned! Suddenly I want to go home as quickly as possible. I have to tell Emily all this! I jump on my bike and sprint towards the exit.

Halfway up the driveway, I approach a black Aston Martin convertible. I recognize the logo on the side of the car. As the car gets closer, I also recognize Edwin, the team boss of the Formula 1 team! He drives past me and waves enthusiastically. In passing, he shouts: "Hey Ronald!"

I don't get the chance to say something back. He changes gears and pushes the throttle. I press my brakes, stand still, and look back.

In the distance I see him park his car and get out. Hank walks over to him. They hug each other enthusiastically. Like true friends.

Only then does the penny drop. *Faster* Racing... Hank *Rapid*...

Damnit!

The Model

The FASTER Model

Speed is an integral part of everything we do. Digitization, internet, mobile phones, and software have made our lives faster.

Many people and organizations struggle to keep up in this rapidly changing world. We are under pressure to innovate faster, but the work culture is risk-averse. We don't have enough time to do our work, but we stack our workday with long meetings. We don't have the information we need, but we are buried in emails, PowerPoints, and reports.

Leaders and teams are frustrated while the best talent is scared away to companies that do better.

This is why we urgently need to redesign our organizations to get more speed. The fastest wins, and not only in Formula 1. Speed has become a crucial competence for survival in a rapidly changing world. But how?

A lot is already known about speed. This book is packed with plenty of theories, models, and solutions to increase speed as part of the story of Ronald and Kitchen Quick. To make explicit the framework the story touched on, we wrote this last chapter. We have listed six elements that help organizations become faster.

Sometimes speed has a negative connotation: high work pressure, stress, poor quality, dissatisfied customers, cutting corners, and proceeding in a hurry. "If you are in a hurry, you will never get there," as the saying goes. However, we don't need to look at speed in this way. Extreme speed can have a significantly positive effect on quality, output, and customer satisfaction. Wanting to be extremely fast forces you to work a lot smarter because working harder doesn't help.

The core of the model underneath the story is that it is not really about speed at all. Speed is constant when you don't do anything.

Newton's first law deals with this: if the sum of the forces on an object is zero, then the acceleration is zero. An object then moves at a constant speed in a straight line (or stands still).

So if you want a higher speed, you have to add a force, do the extra effort, in order to accelerate. Acceleration automatically leads to a higher speed. In other words, don't focus on speed, but focus on going faster!

Therefore the model consists of six parts, the initial letters together form the word "FASTER":

- **F**ocus and clarity – a clear and inspiring goal that works as a compass

- **A**ccelerate decisions – reversible decisions and distributed authority

- **S**implify – the art of omission and simplification

- **T**eam engagement – intrinsic motivation, autonomy, and ownership

- **E**lementary physics – the age-old basic laws for speed and acceleration

- **R**hythmic learning – learn through a cadence of recurring interaction moments

Focus and Clarity

irst to consider is that speed is not everything. Mahatma Gandhi once said: "Speed is irrelevant if you are going in the wrong direction." The right direction is crucial if an organization wants to accelerate fundamentally. In fast organizations, almost all decisions are made in teams and by individuals that are in close contact with the customer because these teams have the most knowledge and information about the customer and the work. For this to succeed, a clear purpose is required. Why are we here? What is our higher goal as an organization? What is our definition of success? When teams have a clear answer to these questions, it becomes easy for them to consider whether a choice helps them get closer or further away from their target. Without a clear direction, teams may start drifting, which is at the expense of acceleration. Make the overarching goal both measurable and inspiring. Purpose statements that are mainly focused on profit margin or shareholder value do not lead to people coming to work full of energy.

In the story of Kitchen Quick, this is mainly reflected with the focus of the racing team. They constantly ask the question: "Does it make the car go faster?" That's the "true North" of a racing team. It offers a compass for daily decisions. By repeating that question often, it will become ingrained and everyone's second nature. This clear direction was missing within Kitchen Quick. One department wanted to sell as much as possible, the other wanted to please the customer as much as possible, and a third one wanted everything to be done according to planning. With such diverse directions, employees are in each other's way. Only when Ronald (through the action of Hank) started to focus on delivery speed and introduced a customer focus, did a common direction arise.

Formula 1 teams are lucky in the sense that it is easy to define such a clear goal. Also, they know exactly where they stand in relation to that goal after every race. In organizations, this is often less obvious. But it is not impossible. This is why the fastest organizations spend a lot of time ensuring that every team and employee knows how their work contributes to the collective goal of the organization. This inspires and motivates enormously.

In the story, Ronald steals an idea from Formula 1: the mandatory Monday morning meeting where the team captain explains what happened during the race, and what that means for the priorities until the next race. This is not a one-sided monologue, but any questions employees may have can be asked and answered. In the intermediate period, people don't have to ask what they should do because they already know what the right thing to do is. It creates a shared consciousness. Everyone simply acts from their expertise and role, with the right context and information. This is not unique to Formula 1; fast business organizations do the same.

It is crucial to be transparent about the joint direction and the progress towards it. And often this transparency goes even further: all information becomes visible and accessible to everyone. Including business performance, finances, roles, compensation, and the like. Only when all relevant information and a clear direction are available, can teams manage themselves.

Ensure a clear purpose, clarity about who has what role, and who has which decision rights. People naturally want to do the right thing and contribute to the purpose. In organizations with a lack of clarity, you see many meetings to coordinate. This is supplemented by many emails with dozens of people cc'd, hoping that they will involve the right people and do the right thing. But hope is not a strategy!

Accelerate Decisions

An important decelerator in organizations is decision making. In many traditional organizations, the typical assumption is that you are not allowed to do anything until you have received permission. This is based on the belief that the best way to reduce risk is by centralizing decision-making authority to a select group of smart people: managers and directors. But they are often unable to oversee the necessity and practical consequences. This, in turn, leads to additional questions or reports. When asking for permission, the responsibility shifts from the requestor to the provider. So the latter wants to make sure they don't miss anything and want to ensure that in case of problems they have a good explanation.

People therefore often lack the authority to properly fulfill their role. Some people think that's fine too, because the responsibility does not lie with them but with the person who decides.

This is especially true when asking another department for permission. They often don't want to take that responsibility at all and don't even need what is requested. In those cases, "no" is a much easier answer than "yes." With a "no," you run no risk. The responsibility remains with the requestor. Thus, decisions in traditional organizations often take a very long time and sometimes escalate to the highest hierarchical levels before decisions are actually made. Often causing a lot of noise along the way. And in the worst case, when a decision has finally been made, the usefulness and necessity have already become obsolete because of the delay.

In the story of Kitchen Quick, this is reflected in the discussions between the different department managers. For example, Paul and his sales team do not want to be responsible for making blueprints, but others still want him to keep that responsibility, even when everyone agrees that salesmen are not trained to do this work. Ronald discovers through the decision tree (which he receives from Hank) that decisions are often reversible. That was an important insight for him. In the story, he makes this thinking step faster than his managers. This makes sense because the existence of their job in the organization to some extent depends on their personal decision-making authority. At one point, Ronald even goes so far as to actually distribute all authority to the employees, resulting in the escalation with the machines. But even then the story shows that individual contributors (folks whose role doesn't involve managing people), Nelson in this case, often make very good and well-founded decisions. Employees deserve that trust. In the end of the story, Kitchen Quick links a customer directly to a team. They figure everything out themselves, with almost no rules or limits.

In this dynamic and rapidly changing world, fast organizations realize that the biggest risk is that they become too slow to act. That's why they hold the opposite assumption: everyone has the freedom and autonomy to realize the goal and purpose of the organization. This means that people are allowed to do anything unless there is a rule that restricts freedom (for good reasons). They trust the positive intent and judgment of the people doing the work. Decision-making authority is moved as much as possible to teams and individuals on the edge of the organization (where there is direct contact with the customer), and where the right information is available. The less permission a team has to request, the faster they become. Thus it is useful to explicitly define the boundaries within decisions can be made. For example, what is the maximum amount a team can decide to indemnify a customer? And how do they get approval for anything above that amount? Make sure to set these limits a bit too wide rather than too tight.

In his book *Turn the Ship Around*, David Marquet explains how he radically improved the culture in a submarine after adjusting his management style. He vowed to never give another order, but instead work with "intent." Every time someone came to ask for permission, he responded with: "What do you intend to do?", "What do you think my decision would be?" and "Is this the right thing to do now?" This caused his people to start thinking about the intentions and possible consequences of their intended actions.

Fast organizations make a conscious choice about how decisions are made, depending on the situation and the type of decision. For example, Sociocratic decision making is based on consent, which uses the principle of "no objection." In other words: a decision is ratified when none of the people present have meaningful or paramount objections. As a participant you don't have to be in favor of the proposal; the only thing that is asked is whether you are perhaps against it. If you are against it, you provide arguments why.

To accelerate, it is important to learn quickly. Discovering what works and what doesn't work, as soon as possible. Making mistakes has become an important precondition for acceleration. Because whoever makes the most mistakes in the shortest amount of time learns the fastest and wins.

It is crucial to offer a safe environment in which people are allowed to make mistakes. The best Formula 1 teams have a strong "no-blame" culture. In the book *Performance* at the Limit, former engineer at Ferrari F1, Rob Smedley, is quoted: "When you have a blame culture, people spend 60-90% of the effort covering what they have done rather than understanding the problem, making the car go quicker." And Paddy Lowe (former technical director Mercedes F1) adds: "Every time you have a negative response to an issue, you're denying yourself the opportunity to improve."

To summarize: decide quickly and see if it works. If yes, keep it. If not, try something else. So it helps to ask yourself: is this decision "good enough for now, safe enough to try?" instead of "is it perfect?"

Simplify

ize reduction enables acceleration immediately. This is why athletes carefully monitor their weight and fat percentage. The same applies to organizations. Big makes slow and inert. From a distance, it sometimes seems that many organizations suffer from a chronic form of obesity. In the HBR article "Do you know how bureaucratic your organization is?" Dr. Gary Hamel measures the costs of bureaucracy on the basis of BMI (*bureaucracy mass index*).[1] He distinguishes seven categories:

1. Bloat: too many managers, administrators, and management layers

2. Friction: too much busywork that slows down decision making

3. Insularity: too much time spent on internal issues

4. Disempowerment: too much constrained autonomy

5. Risk Aversion: too many barriers to risk taking

6. Inertia: too many impediments to proactive change

7. Politics: too much energy devoted to gaining power and influence

---

[1] Gary Hamel, *Harvard Business Review*, "Assessment: Do You Know How Bureaucratic Your Organization Is?", www.bit.ly/2rmU9rx

It is essential to scale down. Fewer people in a team, fewer customers at the same time, fewer offerings, services or products, doing less work at the same time, less bureaucracy and rules: less is more. A reduction in bureaucracy will immediately lead to acceleration. Rules can often be a lot simpler if you start from a place of trust instead of mistrust. As soon as a problem occurs, we tend to add a procedure or policy to prevent it from ever happening again. We often forget that procedures and policies quickly become irrelevant, forming a sort of organizational weight that drags us down in the long run.

A large number of departments are present in the Kitchen Quick story. But only a fraction of the people actually look outside and think from the perspective of the customer. People are mainly concerned with themselves and with each other, while the actual customer value (an installed kitchen) is created across departments. The solution in the story appears to be, among other things, to work in small multidisciplinary teams that help one customer at a time and deliver the result before they go to the next customer. Do less in parallel and reduce the number of departments that serve each other. Work sequentially and serve one customer at a time as much as possible.

Do we need to centralize or decentralize customer service, planning, purchasing, sales? At Kitchen Quick, the solution was decentralization. But that is not always the case. Sometimes it makes perfect sense to centralize something. It is not a question of right or wrong; both situations have advantages and disadvantages. So with these types of design choices always think about the question: which of the two allows us to deliver value to our customer faster?

To accelerate, it is therefore important to keep a constant focus on simplification. The art of omission. Pick up one thing at a time, simplify it, and then move on to the next. Ask customers and employees where they see opportunities for simplification. They are confronted with this on a daily basis and are therefore an important source of inspiration for acceleration. And it's usually in the little things. Requesting for permission needlessly, delivering a report that nobody looks at, having to click <OK> five times in a system where one time would be sufficient, and so on. Work from the basis of trust and common sense among employees and customers, and enable them to do their work as well as possible.

Oftentimes this is not easy: simplifying something is much more difficult than making something complex. Remove things that were once invented for a good reason and see if those reasons still apply. And when in doubt: throw it away and see if you miss it. You can always add it again.

Team Engagement

The fastest organizations are built out of self-organizing, multidisciplinary teams. Teams that can deliver value autonomously and steer themselves without depending on others. They contain all the required skills and are in direct contact with the customer and receive feedback on their results directly. When those ingredients are present, enthusiasm and positive energy naturally emerge. In his book *Drive*, Daniel Pink explains three factors that help to unlock intrinsic motivation: autonomy, mastery, and purpose. Everyone has a deep desire to have the freedom to determine how to work, to develop skills and get better, and to be able to work on something meaningful. If employees are disengaged, take a closer look at how they have been treated by the organization, instead of blaming the people.

The idea of self-organizing multidisciplinary teams is not new at all. In fact, this idea has been applied in many organizations for decades, even in organizations with a very strong hierarchy. Because, what happens if there is a large and unclear problem that must be solved as fast as possible? Then they form a task force, crisis team, war room, or something similar. These consist of people from all departments so that all knowledge, skills, and decision rights are present. These people are freed from other work and are given the full mandate to solve the problem. If it is important and must be done quickly, we've already known for a long time how to do it: multidisciplinary self-managing teams. So if it always has to be very fast, then let the entire organization consist of teams of this kind.

This is exactly the solution in the Kitchen Quick story. Ronald just keeps running into the walls between departments. The final piece of the puzzle is to create customer teams that measure, produce, and install a kitchen from start to finish. Such teams deliver a kitchen within a week. By striving for efficiency, departments in many organizations are going to optimize themselves. On paper, the internal KPIs look great. But that optimization leads to ping-pong between departments and longer lead times. At the expense of the customer! The key to extreme acceleration and agility in organizations lies in removing interdependencies. Ronald applies this by transforming the departments into competence areas and putting the self-organizing and self-learning teams at the center. And they are very focused on their own customers.

Good teams have all the required skills and competencies. Collaboration skills become extra important. Egos, star players, and self-appointed gods do not belong in such teams. The team is always more important than the individual. Good teams also recognize that everyone has talents and disabilities. And the handicap of one is sometimes the talent of the other. And that is fine because the joint talent of the team counts.

Every person is different and has a "user manual" to working with them, and we usually only discover their manual when we work with someone for a long time. We can speed up this process if you write your own user manual and share it with the team. Consider these questions: What energizes you? What drives you crazy? Which traits do you value most in others? What is something that people often misunderstand about you? What is the best way to communicate with you?

What is the best way to convince you of something? How would you like to receive feedback?[2]

In traditional organizations, there is often a fixed set of tasks and responsibilities, rooted in a job description. If you want to develop yourself within this system, you have to wait for a promotion or for the opportunity to switch jobs. This is a huge limiting factor in the potential of people and the organization. Fast organizations let go of functions and enable people to hold a mix of roles. People choose which roles they want to take on (autonomy) based on the competence they want to develop (mastery) and the contribution they think they can make to the higher goal of the organization (purpose). This results in a dynamic marketplace of roles, teams, and projects that people can sign up for. In Formula 1 you can see this at pit stops. Once the race is over, the people in the pit stop team have different roles and responsibilities to fulfill.

---

[2] Adam Bryant, The New York Times, "Want To Know Me? Just Read My User Manual," www.nyti.ms/2M5KXCn

Elementary Physics

lementary physics has already laid down the basic laws for speed and acceleration. They are laws, so you cannot turn them on or off. We apply them every day. We have already explained Newton's first law in the run-up to this chapter. It teaches that it's not about speed, but about acceleration.

The formula for speed confirms this: $v(t) = v(o) + at$. The speed at time t is the speed at time o (the current speed of an object) plus a times t (acceleration multiplied by time).

The last part of this formula is particularly interesting: a times t. If acceleration is constant, the speed will continue to increase. So if you accelerate for a long time, you will go faster and faster. Acceleration is also part of Newton's second law: $F = ma$ (force is mass times acceleration). Or put differently: $a = F / m$ (acceleration is power divided by mass). So in order to increase a (acceleration), you have two options: more power, or less mass. Or both, of course. Option 2, in particular, deserves extra attention. With the same force, the acceleration increases when there is less mass. That's why we go on a diet when we want to run faster. The less weight you have, the less force it takes to run.

This is very relevant for organizations. In many cases, they are too heavy, too bloated, and too big, as we have already covered earlier. Reducing mass helps enormously. But increasing strength is also an option. In the story of Kitchen Quick, this is reflected in a stronger engine, a fully automated sawing machine. We've also talked about eliminating counterforces like aerodynamic drag. The less (air) resistance, the faster the car goes. A lot of internal rules and procedures act as counterforces and make things slower.

At the same time, a racing car needs enough downward pressure, downforce, to stick to the tarmac. If you took away all air resistance, the car would have no grip and could even take off into the air! When designing the aerodynamics of a good racing car, the trick is to generate as much downforce as possible through spoilers, with the least possible air resistance. For organizations, this means: ensure the minimum set of rules and boundaries that are needed to enable speed, without slowing you down too much.

In the story of Kitchen Quick, Mark, the driver, mentions the rules of physics. He says something interesting: if you go too slowly into a corner, you have too little downforce and therefore you fly out of the track. In other words: speed is crucial to keep control of a racing car. This phenomenon stems from Newton's third law: "for every action, there is an equal and opposite reaction." High speed provides more control, even if it is sometimes scary.

Another relevant physics law is that of relativity. Albert Einstein's general theory of relativity (also known as Galileo's relativity theory) indicates that absolute speed does not actually exist; speed is relative. This certainly applies in Formula 1. Ultimately it is not so much about absolute speed or acceleration, but about the speed compared to the other cars. The first one to cross the finish line wins. Speed and acceleration must be seen in their context and environment. So look primarily at customers (or the competition) to decide what speed you need.

One more thing. Does your work mainly consist of knowledge work? Are you an information-dense company? Do you work at a bank, government organization, insurer, or consultancy? Then realize that your work outputs few physical components. The work is mainly about information, algorithms, data, or knowledge. And those things don't have any mass! Take a look at Newton's second law: $a = F / m$.

In the absence of mass, the acceleration rises quickly. Perhaps that explains why our society is currently accelerating so strongly. Because digitization has no weight, acceleration is moving towards infinity!

Rhythmic Learning

eal-life data shows that employees on average attend sixty-two meetings per month, and half of those are considered a waste of time. Some managers are in meetings from early morning until late at night; they have no time left to do actual work. Therefore, it is no surprise that during the meeting people often work on their laptops, use their phone, or just stare out the window.

Extremely fast organizations cannot afford this waste of energy. Instead, they take great care to design a fit for purpose meeting structure. Each meeting has a specific purpose, an associated structure, and duration. The meetings interlock and create a fixed cadence that works as a whole to bring the work forward.

In his book *Death by Meeting*, Patrick Lencioni describes the following meeting cadence:

- A *five-minute daily* (standing) check-in meeting to coordinate the intended results for that day and to remove any blockages.

- A *weekly tactical* of forty-five minutes to an hour and a half in which weekly activities and metrics are reviewed and tactical obstacles are resolved.

- A *monthly strategy meeting* of two to four hours in which important issues are examined and a discussion about topics that affect long-term success.

- A *quarterly off-site review day* for team development and in which strategy, competition, and industry trends are examined.

Are you overloaded by recurring meetings that are not working properly? Then it is sometimes best to just cancel all meetings for a week or two. You will soon find out what you really miss. Then you can rebuild your rhythm from the ground up.

Another example of a framework with an explicit meeting structure is scrum. In scrum the plans are made by the people who do the work themselves and people learn by doing. An important meeting in scrum, for example, is the Sprint Retrospective: the team meets after each sprint to reflect and determine what can be improved in the next period. Even if you don't use scrum, a regular retrospective can be very valuable. Slow down to then be able to speed up again. In other words: slow down, or you'll never get there!

Formula 1 teams use a very disciplined rhythm of around fifty meetings per race weekend with a clear focus on learning and improving. The all-hands meeting in the factory is another example that Ronald implemented immediately. Although he forgets that in order for that to work, he needs input. Only later does he introduce the team meeting on Friday, which looks like a Sprint Retrospective. Ronald is very clear about the importance of this rhythm and he is consciously making it "mandatory." A lot can be said about the way he does that. However, in his role as managing director, he is very decisive: the rhythm is key, and no exceptions are made, no matter how difficult that can be sometimes. Such discipline brings an organization into a fixed cadence. This cadence prevents ad hoc coordination and offers high-frequency results: an important precondition for acceleration. It is crucial to maintain that rhythm in a disciplined manner. A fixed rhythm creates predictability. It creates a clear "landing place" for unforeseen events. When it is crystal clear when which topics are being discussed and in what way, we do not have to waste energy figuring out how to communicate. It goes automatically. Whatever happens, there is always a moment of interaction nearby.

To be able to learn quickly, the trick is to make the "cycle time" as short as possible so that you can learn whether it works or where adjustments are needed. The shorter this cycle time is, the more experiments we can launch to learn. This is why IT teams automate repetitive work, with the positive side effect of reducing the chance of human error. This is why Amazon can roll out improvements to its website every minute. This is similar to Formula 1 teams: with their extremely short cycle time, they deliver and test improvements to the car very quickly. So it is not really about the time to market, but about the time to learn.

In many organizations, people don't start work without a plan; they only receive a budget based on detailed cost and revenue planning, and the expectation is to proceed according to plan. Deviation from the plan is not permitted or leads to corrective action. We try to predict the future and hold on to it tightly, but the future cannot be captured in plans. In today's fast-changing world, most problems are too complex for a plan to be able to solve. Fast organizations know that it makes no sense to put a lot of energy into making detailed plans that look far ahead. Instead, they anchor short-cycle planning in their daily rhythm.

It is important to find a balance between the short-term and the long-term. For example, during the course of a season, Formula 1 teams will shift the focus of a third of their staff to develop the car of the following season. These people remain part of the overall team but have time to try out more extreme innovations, for which there is no time in the teams that work on small, incremental improvements. Make sure that the cadence creates space for both short-term improvements (evolution) and more uncertain initiatives that have a long-term focus (revolution).

The same is true for changing the organization. With astonishment, we have heard a management team say: "We have decided not to reorganize in the coming year because that always causes so much hassle and unrest. But after a while, we do have to shake things up again to make it work again." If you only do (huge) organizational changes every once in a while, it is no surprise it causes unrest. Fast organizations, on the other hand, understand that in a world where change is the only constant, the trick is to change faster than your environment. That is why they create an organization that constantly changes themselves, in small steps, with input from the people who do the work.

Hungry Minds
(Further Reading)

While preparing and writing this story and creating the model, we were inspired by a large number of books, articles, videos, and people. To mention everything here in great detail is impossible. If you want to continue reading, a few tips follow below.

Formula 1

Mark Jenkins, Ken Pasternak & Richard West, *Performance at the Limit. Business Lessons from Formula 1 Motor Racing*. Cambridge University Press, 2016

Ross Brawn & Adam Parr, *Total Competition. Lessons in Strategy from Formula One*. Simon and Schuster, 2016

David Coulthard, *The Winning Formula: Leadership, Strategy and Motivation the F1 Way*. Blink Publishing, 2018

Mark Gallagher, *The Business of Winning: Strategic Success from the Formula One Track to the Boardroom*. Kogan Page, 2014

Management and organization

Aaron Dignan, *Brave New Work. Are You Ready to Reinvent Your Organization?* Portfolio Penguin, 2019

Brian M. Carney & Isaac Getz, *Freedom Inc. How Corporate Liberation Unleashes Employee Potential and Business Performance.* Somme Valley House, 2016

Frederic Laloux, *Reinventing Organizations.* Nelson Parker, 2014

Ricardo Semler, *Maverick: The Success Story Behind the World's Most Unusual Workplace.* Grand Central Publishing, 1995

Nassim Nicholas Taleb, *Antifragile: Things That Gain from Disorder.* Random House, 2014

Change management

Patrick Lencioni, *Getting Naked – A Business Fable About Shedding The Three Fears That Sabotage Client Loyalty.* John Wiley & Sons, 2010

Jason Little, *Lean Change Management: Innovative practices for managing organizational change.* Happy Melly Express, 2014

Gene Kim, Kevin Behr, George Spafford, *The Phoenix Project: A Novel about IT, DevOps, and Helping Your Business Win.* IT Revolution Press, 2018

John P. Kotter and Holger Rathgeber, *Our Iceberg Is Melting: Changing and Succeeding Under Any Conditions.* Penguin Random House, 2016

Malcolm Gladwell, *The Tipping Point: How Little Things Can Make a Big Difference.* Back Bay Books, 2002

Leadership

David Marquet, *Turn the Ship Around! A True Story of Turning Followers into Leaders.* Portfolio, 2013

Daniel Pink, *Drive: The Surprising Truth About What Motivates Us*. Riverhead Books, 2009

Edgar H. Schein, *Humble Inquiry: The Gentle Art of Asking instead of Telling*. Berett-Koehler Publishers, 2013

Patrick Lencioni, *The Five Dysfunctions of a Team: A Leadership Fable*. Jossey-Bass, 2011

Peter F. Drucker, *The Effective Executive: The Definitive Guide to Getting the Right Things Done*. Harper Business Essentials, 2006

Rini van Solingen, *How to lead self-managing teams?: A business novel on changing leadership from sheepherding to beekeeping*. CreateSpace Independent Publishing Platform, 2016

Stephen Denning, *The Leader's Guide to Radical Management: Reinventing the Workplace for the 21st Century*. Jossey Bass, 2010

Eric Ries, *The Lean Startup: How Today's Entrepreneurs Use Continuous Innovation to Create Radically Successful Businesses*. Currency, 2011

Meetings & decision making

Patrick Lencioni, *Death by Meeting: A Leadership Fable...about Solving the Most Painful Problem in Business*. John Wiley & Sons Inc., 2004

Ted J. Rau & Jerry Koch-Gonzalez, *Many Voices One Song: Shared Power with Sociocracy*. Institute for Peaceable Communities Inc., 2018

Brian J. Robertson, *Holacracy: The New Management System for a Rapidly Changing World*. Henry Holt, 2015

Jeff Sutherland, Rini van Solingen and Eelco Rustenburg,
The Power of Scrum. CreateSpace, 2011

Agility

Stephen Denning, The Age of Agile: How Smart Companies Are
Transforming the Way Work Gets Done. AMACOM, 2018

John P. Kotter, Accelerate: Building Strategic Agility for a Faster-
Moving World. Harvard Business Review Press, 2014

Stanley McChrystal, Team of Teams: New Rules of Engagement
for a Complex World. Portfolio, 2015

Jeff Sutherland and Jeff Sutherland Jr., Scrum: The Art of
Doing Twice the Work in Half the Time. Currency, 2014

Ken Schwaber and Jeff Sutherland, Software in 30 Days:
How Agile Managers Beat the Odds, Delight Their Customers,
and Leave Competitors in the Dust. Wiley, 2012

Acknowledgements

Creating a book is teamwork. And not only from us as authors but also from a large group of people around us. That is why we want to take this opportunity to thank a number of people.

Most of the ideas in this book were invented by others. We owe a debt to the countless pioneers and other brave people who have developed these ways of working and have shaped our thinking about organizations.

Svenja de Vos, thank you for your intense reviews of multiple versions of this manuscript. Your input has contributed to a much sharper formation of the main characters and has ensured that Emily is no longer a "bitch" and Ronald much less an "asshole". ;-) Thank you very much for your sharp and clear feedback and for all your enthusiasm about this book!

The reviewers of this book: Rob Dielissen, Klaas Gosink, Stèphanie Gosink, Evert-Jan van der Kleij, Hans de Man, Marten Meij, and Wilbert Seele, for your critical comments and Marten in particular for his refinement of race details in the story.

Luuk Snellen and Wilco van Meijl from kitchen and interior designer Willuks (www.willuks.nl) for a peek behind the scenes of the production process of custom-made kitchens.

Bart de Vaan and Rob Heymann, who invited Jurriaan in 2017 for a tour behind the scenes of Red Bull Racing. This is where the interest in the organizational dimension of Formula 1 was ignited. Many thanks for that!

Mark Jenkins, Ken Pasternak, and Richard West for writing *Performance at the Limit: Business Lessons from Formula 1 Motor Racing*. A book that has given us a golden glimpse behind the scenes of Formula 1.

Harry Brouwer, Frank Coster, Frans van der Horst, Anneke Keller, MariClle Lichtenberg, Huub Vermeulen, and Svenja de Vos, for your praising words. You made us proud and almost made us blush.

All colleagues at The Ready, TU-Delft, and Prowareness. Knowledge and ideas always arise through interaction with others. Whether it's at the coffee machine or during projects at customers', it doesn't matter. Thanks for all the cooperation and inspiration.

Tim Casasola for your awesome editing skills and org design knowledge that helped create this book. And Tom Nixon for being our British sparring partner.

Nadine Kamer for your expert advice and feedback during the narration and production of the audiobook.

Jesse Krieger and his team at Lifestyle Entrepreneurs Press for making the English language edition a reality. And Lee Constantine of Publishizer for introducing us to Jesse.

Thank you to both our home fronts. Writing a book takes time. And even though that work sometimes takes place at the kitchen table, physical presence in that case means mental absence. Thank you for your time, support, and understanding!

Last but not least, thank you to Janine Sloof and Sandra Wouters. At the beginning of 2018, you came up with the surprising idea for a management book with a connection to Formula 1. That was the very first spark for this book. Without your idea and initiative, this book would not have been there.

Jurriaan Kamer and Rini van Solingen
Delft, The Netherlands, October 31st, 2019

Jurriaan Kamer

SPEAKER | ORGANIZATION DESIGNER | CHANGE AGENT

"The tension between organizations optimized for predictability and the unpredictable world they inhabit has reached a breaking point. Organizations built on 'sense and respond' instead of 'plan and predict' are the future."

ABOUT
Jurriaan is an expert in the field of organizing differently. He is obsessed with modern organizations and how you can transform an existing organization. He studied companies like Spotify, Apple, Google, Facebook, and Airbnb to discover how they work. In addition, he has been a fan and visitor of Formula 1 for years. When he was given the opportunity to look behind the scenes of Formula 1, the inspiration for this book was laid.

SPEAKING
Jurriaan offers keynote presentations and workshops that inspire change and create the right mindset and context for your event, full of real-life examples from Jurriaan's research on the future of work and 21st century organizations. His signature speech *"How to make your organization as fast and agile as a Formula 1 team"* has been received by audiences across the world.

TRANSFORMATIONS
Jurriaan is a Partner at The Ready, an organization design and transformation agency focused on the future of work (more info on the right).

STAY INSPIRED
Jurriaan has written several popular articles, such as "How to build your own Spotify model" and "Beyond Agile: Why agile has not fixed your problems." Follow him on LinkedIn or Twitter (@jurriaankamer) and subscribe at newsletter.jurriaankamer.com to receive a stream of interesting articles.

More info: www.jurriaankamer.com
Contact directly: jurriaan@formula-x.co

Rini van Solingen

SPEAKER | AUTHOR | PROFESSOR | ENTREPRENEUR

Expert in speed and agility of people and organizations.

"We face an era of organizational Darwinism: the ones that will survive are the ones that adapt and adjust themselves best to their changing environment."

SPEAKING

Rini is an engaged speaker about the speed and agility of people and organizations. His talent is to explain complex content in a simple, energetic, and humorous way. He does this by using simple analogies and by telling concrete practical anecdotes. He also shares simple and powerful models in his presentations.

WORKSHOPS & TRAINING

A lecture by Rini usually lasts an hour. However, sometimes there is a need for a longer talk or more intensive interaction. In this case, a workshop or training is a great alternative. Workshops usually last 2 to 3 hours and are designed to give the best results. Training by Rini is also possible, varying from one to a few days or, for example, half a day per month for six months in a row. Please contact Rini to discuss this option.

WRITING

Rini is the author of a number of management books, including *The Power of Scrum* (2011 - with Jeff Sutherland and Eelco Rustenburg), *Scrum for Managers* (2015 — with Rob van Lanen) and the management novel: *How to lead self-managing teams?* (2016).

More info: www.rinivansolingen.com
Contact directly: rini@formula-x.co

SPEED AND AGILITY OF PEOPLE AND ORGANIZATIONS.

www.rinivansolingen.com

CPSIA information can be obtained
at www.ICGtesting.com
Printed in the USA
LVHW081300060220
646073LV00007B/38/J